THE TYNDALE
NEW TESTAMENT COMMENTARIES

LEON MORRIS

General Editor

EPHESIANS

An Introduction and Commentary

Francis Foulkes

IVP Academic

An imprint of InterVarsity Press
Downers Grove, Illinois

Inter-Varsity Press

Nottingham, England

InterVarsity Press, USA
P.O. Box 1400, Downers Grove, IL 60515-1426, USA
World Wide Web: www.ivpress.com
Email: email@ivpress.com

Inter-Varsity Press, England
Norton Street, Nottingham NG7 3HR, England
Website: www.ivpbooks.com
Email: ivp@ivpbooks.com

InterVarsity Press®, USA, is the book-publishing division of InterVarsity Christian Fellowship/USA®, a student movement active on campus at hundreds of universities, colleges and schools of nursing in the United States of America, and a member movement of the International Fellowship of Evangelical Students. For information about local and regional activities, write Public Relations Dept., InterVarsity Christian Fellowship/USA, 6400 Schroeder Rd., P.O. Box 7895, Madison, WI 53707-7895, or visit the IVCF website at <www.intervarsity.org>.

Inter-Varsity Press, England, is closely linked with the Universities and Colleges Christian Fellowship, a student movement connecting Christian Unions in universities and colleges throughout Great Britain, and a member movement of the International Fellowship of Evangelical Students. Website: www.uccf.org.uk.

USA ISBN: 978-0-8308-2989-7
UK ISBN: 978-0-85111-879-6

Set in Palatino
Typeset in Great Britain by Parker Typesetting Service, Leicester

Printed in the United States of America ∞

Library of Congress Cataloging-in-Publication Data

Foulkes, Francis.
  [Epistle of Paul to the Ephesians]
  Ephesians : an introduction and commentary / Francis Foulkes.
    p. cm.—(The Tyndale New Testament commentaries ; 10)
  Includes bibliographical references.
  ISBN 978-0-8308-2989-7 (pbk. : alk. paper)—ISBN 978-0-85111-879-6
(pbk. : alk. paper)
1. Bible. N.T. Ephesians—Commentaries. I. Title.
  BS2695.53.F68 2007
  227'.507—dc22

                              2007004430

British Library Cataloguing in Publication Data

Foulkes, Francis, 1926
  The Letter of Paul to the Ephesians. 2nd ed.
  1. Bible. N.T. Ephesians. English Revised
  standard. Critical studies
  I. Title.   II. Series
  227'.506

P	19	18	17	16	15	14	13	12	11	10	9	8	7	6	5	4	3	2
Y	23	22	21	20	19	18	17	16	15	14	13	12	11	10	09	08	07

GENERAL PREFACE

The original *Tyndale Commentaries* aimed at providing help for the general reader of the Bible. They concentrated on the meaning of the text without going into scholarly technicalities. They sought to avoid 'the extremes of being unduly technical or unhelpfully brief'. Most who have used the books agree that there has been a fair measure of success in reaching that aim.

Times, however, change. A series that has served so well for so long is perhaps not quite as relevant as it was when it was first launched. New knowledge has come to light. The discussion of critical questions has moved on. Bible-reading habits have changed. When the original series was commenced it could be presumed that most readers used the Authorized Version and one's comments were made accordingly, but this situation no longer obtains.

The decision to revise and up-date the whole series was not reached lightly, but in the end it was thought that this is what is required in the present situation. There are new needs, and they will be better served by new books or by a thorough up-dating of the old books. The aims of the original series remain. The new commentaries are neither minuscule nor unduly long. They are exegetical rather than homiletic. They do not discuss all the critical questions, but none is written without an awareness of the problems that engage the attention of New Testament scholars. Where it is felt that formal consideration should be given to such questions, they are discussed in the Introduction and sometimes in Additional Notes.

But the main thrust of these commentaries is not critical. These books are written to help the non-technical reader understand the Bible better. They do not presume a knowledge of Greek, and all Greek words discussed are transliterated; but the authors have the Greek text before them and their comments are made on the basis of what the originals say. The authors are free to choose their own modern translation, but are asked to bear in mind the variety of translations in current use.

The new series of *Tyndale Commentaries* goes forth, as the former series did, in the hope that God will graciously use these books to help the general reader to understand as fully and clearly as possible the meaning of the New Testament.

LEON MORRIS

CONTENTS

GENERAL PREFACE   5

AUTHOR'S PREFACE TO THE FIRST EDITION   9

PREFACE TO THE SECOND EDITION   11

CHIEF ABBREVIATIONS   13

BIBLIOGRAPHY   15

INTRODUCTION
    The nature and teaching of the letter   19
    Destination   22
    Ephesians and Colossians   25
    Ephesians and other New Testament writings   29
    Arguments for a later date   37
    Other evidence for authorship   40
    The work of an imitator or of the apostle?   44

ANALYSIS   49

COMMENTARY   51

AUTHOR'S PREFACE TO THE FIRST EDITION

Some of the New Testament Epistles have had few outstanding commentaries written on them in English in the past hundred years. This is not so in the case of Ephesians. Our study of this Epistle is enriched by the judicious work of Armitage Robinson, Westcott and Abbott on the Greek text, the invaluable practical expositions of Findlay and Dale, and most of all by the work of Bishop Handley Moule whose work always offers the uncommon combination of careful scholarship and devotional application. To these and others (teachers and preachers as well as writers) I have been indebted constantly, and I realize that this has been the case often where I have not been sufficiently aware of the source of my indebtedness to acknowledge it.

In the Introduction there is some attempt to study briefly the problems associated with the peculiar nature of Ephesians, the Epistle's relationship to other New Testament writings, its authorship and original destination. These questions, however, interesting as they are, appear to be less important for the understanding of this Epistle, than is the case with almost any other New Testament letter. Therefore, I do not regard the Introduction as the most important part of the book. Doctrinal teaching is given in the Epistle without the direct application to the problems of a particular situation which we find in an Epistle such as Galatians; we have moral precepts without that reference to the peculiar problems of a church which we have in the Corinthian Epistles. Therefore, it is the study of the language and thought of the Epistle itself that will lead us most deeply into the writer's understanding of the glory of God in Christ and of the high calling of those who themselves have come to live in him. Sir Edwin Hoskyns once asked, 'Can we study a language, and awake to the Truth? Can we bury ourselves in a lexicon, and arise in the presence of God?' Many have found that they can indeed in the case of the words of this Epistle, which Coleridge called 'one of the divinest compositions of man'.

FRANCIS FOULKES

PREFACE TO THE
SECOND EDITION

When the first edition of this Commentary was written nearly twenty-five years ago, I commented on the wealth of outstanding writings on Ephesians. The time since then has seen the publication of further significant works in English, the major two-volume work by Markus Barth in the *Anchor Bible* and others in standard series, including those of F. F. Bruce (*New International Commentary on the New Testament*), G. B. Caird (*New Clarendon Bible*), J. L. Houlden (*Pelican New Testament Commentary*) and C. L. Mitton (*New Century Bible*). The work of John R. W. Stott, *The Message of Ephesians* (*The Bible Speaks Today* series) offers a fine blend of attention to exegetical detail and concern for application of the teaching of Ephesians to our contemporary situation.

There have been important studies on the background to the letter; in J. C. Kirby's *Ephesians, Baptism and Pentecost* there is a stress on the liturgical, in other works close comparison with the language of Qumran or the language and thought of Gnosticism. Scholarly opinion continues to be divided on the question of the authorship of the letter and, for the most part, recent works offer only a fresh arrangement of the old arguments one way and the other. A. van Roon has written a major work, *The Authenticity of Ephesians*, defending the Pauline authorship. On the other side, the major new work has been in the form of suggested situations in which the letter may have been composed if it were not Paul's own.

I have tried to grapple afresh with the questions associated with the authorship and original setting and destination. It remains my conviction, however, that these questions are less important for the understanding of this letter than is the case with most other New Testament documents. It is the study of the language and thought of the letter that matters most, as I argued in the preface to the first edition.

This revised edition of the commentary uses the Revised Standard Version as base, but other translations are referred to frequently.

FRANCIS FOULKES

CHIEF ABBREVIATIONS

AV	Authorized Version, 1611.
Barth (*AB*)	M. Barth, *Ephesians* (*Anchor Bible*, 2 vols.; New York, 1974).
Barth (*BW*)	M. Barth, *The Broken Wall* (London, 1960).
BDB	F. Brown, S. R. Driver and C. A. Briggs, *A Hebrew and English Lexicon of the Old Testament* (Oxford, 1976 reprint).
Bruce (*EE*)	F. F. Bruce, *The Epistle to the Ephesians* (London, 1961).
Bruce (*NICNT*)	F. F. Bruce, *The Epistle to the Colossians, to Philemon and to the Ephesians* (*New International Commentary on the New Testament*; Grand Rapids, 1984).
CGT	*Cambridge Greek Testament.*
ET	English translation.
ExpT	*Expository Times.*
Goodspeed (*KE*)	E. J. Goodspeed, *The Key to Ephesians* (Chicago, 1956).
Goodspeed (*ME*)	E. J. Goodspeed, *The Meaning of Ephesians* (Chicago, 1933).
JSNT	*Journal for the Study of the New Testament.*
JTS	*Journal of Theological Studies.*
LS	H. G. Liddell and R. S. Scott, *A Greek-English Lexicon*, new edition revised by H. S. Jones and R. Mackenzie, 2 vols. (Oxford, 1940).
LXX	The Septuagint (pre-Christian Greek version of the Old Testament).
Mitton (*EE*)	C. L. Mitton, *The Epistle to the Ephesians: Its Authorship, Origin and Purpose* (Oxford, 1951).

Mitton (*NCB*)	C. L. Mitton, *Ephesians* (*New Century Bible*; London, 1976).
Moffatt	J. Moffatt, *A New Translation of the Bible*, 1913.
Moule (*CB*)	H. C. G. Moule, *Commentary on Ephesians* (*Cambridge Bible*; Cambridge, 1884).
Moule (*ES*)	H. C. G. Moule, *Ephesian Studies* (London, 1900).
MS (S)	Manuscript(s)
NEB	New English Bible, NT 1961, ²1970; OT 1970.
NIV	New International Version, 1973, 1978, 1984.
NTS	*New Testament Studies.*
Phillips	J. B. Phillips, *The New Testament in Modern English*, 1958.
RSV	Revised Standard Version, NT 1946, ²1971; OT 1952.
RV	Revised Version, 1881.
Sampley (*PC*)	J. P. Sampley, 'The Letter to the Ephesians' in *Ephesians, Colossians, 2 Thessalonians, the Pastoral Epistles* (*Proclamation Commentaries*; Philadelphia, 1978).
TDNT	*Theological Dictionary of the New Testament*, edited by G. Kittel and G. Friedrich (ET, Grand Rapids, 1964–74).
TEV	Today's English Version, 1966.
UBS	United Bible Societies.
Weymouth	R. F. Weymouth, *The New Testament in Modern Speech*, 1903.

BIBLIOGRAPHY

Abbott, T. K., *The Epistle to the Ephesians and to the Colossians* (*International Critical Commentary*; Edinburgh, 1897).

Allan, J. A., *The Epistle to the Ephesians* (*Torch Bible Commentaries*; London, 1959).

Barclay, W., *Commentary on Galatians and Ephesians* (*Daily Study Bible*; Edinburgh, 1954).

Barth, M., *The Broken Wall* (London, 1960).

Barth, M., *Ephesians* (*Anchor Bible*, 2 vols.; New York, 1974).

Barry, A., 'The Epistles to the Ephesians, Philippians and Colossians' in *A New Testament Commentary for English Readers*, ed. C. J. Ellicott (1896).

Beare, F. W., 'Ephesians' in *The Interpreter's Bible*, vol. 10 (New York, 1953).

Bengel, J. A., *Gnomon Novi Testamenti* (reprint; Grand Rapids, 1978).

Bruce, F. F., *The Epistle to the Colossians, to Philemon and to the Ephesians* (*New International Commentary on the New Testament*; Grand Rapids, 1984).

Bruce, F. F., *The Epistle to the Ephesians* (London, 1961).

Caird, G. B., *Paul's Letters from Prison* (*New Clarendon Bible*; Oxford, 1976).

Calvin, J., *The Epistles of Paul the Apostle to the Galatians, Ephesians, Philippians and Colossians* (ET; Edinburgh, 1965).

Chadwick, H., 'Ephesians' in *Peake's Commentary on the Bible* (London, 1962).

Conzelmann, H., 'Der Brief an die Epheser' in *Die Kleineren Briefe des Apostels Paulus* (*Das Neue Testament Deutsch*; Göttingen, 1962).

Cross, F. C., *Studies in Ephesians* (London, 1956).

Dale, R. W., *The Epistle to the Ephesians* (London, 1883).

Dibelius, M., and Geeven, H., *An die Kolosser, Epheser an Philemon* (*Handbuch zum Neuen Testament*; Tübingen, 1953).

Dodd, C. H., 'Ephesians' in *The Abingdon Bible Commentary*, ed. by F. C. Eiselen, E. Lewis and D. G. Downey (New York, 1929).

Findlay, G. C., *Commentary on Ephesians* (*Expositor's Bible*; London, 1902).

Gnilka, J., *Der Epheserbrief* (*Theologischer Kommentar zum Neuen Testament*; Freiburg, 1977).

Goodspeed, E. J., *The Key to Ephesians* (Chicago, 1956).

Goodspeed, E. J., *The Meaning of Ephesians* (Chicago, 1933).

Hendriksen, W., *Exposition of Ephesians* (*New Testament Commentary*; Grand Rapids, 1967).

Hodge, C. E., *A Commentary on the Epistle to the Ephesians* (reprint; Grand Rapids, 1950).

Hort, F. J. A., *Prolegomena to St. Paul's Epistles to the Romans and Ephesians* (London, 1895).

Houlden, J. L., *Paul's Letters from Prison* (*Pelican New Testament Commentary*; Harmondsworth, 1970).

Johnston, G., *Ephesians, Philippians, Colossians and Philemon* (*New Century Bible*; London, 1967).

Käsemann, E., 'Ephesians and Acts' in *Studies in Luke-Acts*, ed. by L. E. Keck and J. L. Martyn (London, 1968).

Kirby, J. C., *Ephesians, Baptism and Pentecost* (London, 1968).

Lightfoot, J. B., *Biblical Essays* (London, 1893).

Lincoln, A. T., *Paradise now and not yet* (Cambridge, 1981).

Lock, W., *Commentary on Ephesians* (*Westminster Commentaries*; London, 1929).

Martin, R. P., *Ephesians* (*Broadman Bible Commentary*; Nashville, 1972).

Masson, C., *L'Epitre aux Ephesiens* (*Commentaire du Nouveau Testament*; Paris, 1953).

Mitton, C. L., *Ephesians* (*New Century Bible*; London, 1976).

Mitton, C. L., *The Epistle to the Ephesians: Its Authorship, Origin and Purpose* (Oxford, 1951).

Moule, H. C. G., *Commentary on Ephesians* (*Cambridge Bible*; Cambridge, 1884).

Moule, H. C. G., *Ephesian Studies* (London, 1900).

Moulton, H. K., *Colossians, Philemon and Ephesians* (*Epworth's Preachers' Commentaries*; London, 1962).

Murray, J. O. F., *Commentary on Ephesians* (*Cambridge Greek Testament*; Cambridge, 1914).

Percy, E., *Die Probleme der Kolosser – und Epheserbriefe* (Lund, 1946).

Robinson, J. A., *St Paul's Epistle to the Ephesians* (London, 1964).

Roon, A. van, *The Authenticity of Ephesians* (Leiden, 1974).

Salmond, S. D. F., 'The Epistle of Paul to the Ephesians' in *The Expositor's Greek Testament*, vol. 3 (London, 1903).

Sampley, J. P., 'And the two shall become one flesh': A Study of Traditions in Ephesians 5:21–33 (Cambridge, 1971).

Sampley, J. P., 'The Letter to the Ephesians' in *Ephesians, Colossians, 2 Thessalonians, the Pastoral Epistles* (*Proclamation Commentaries*; Philadelphia, 1978).

Schlier, H., *Der Brief an die Epheser: Ein Commentar* (Dusseldorf, 1957).

Schnackenburg, R., *Der Brief an die Epheser* (*Evangelisch-Katholischer Kommentar zum Neuen Testament*; Neukirchen-Vluyn, 1982).

Scott, E. F., *The Epistles to the Colossians, to Philemon and to the Ephesians* (*Moffatt New Testament Commentary*; London, 1930).

Simpson, E. K., 'The Epistle to the Ephesians' in E. K. Simpson and F. F. Bruce, *The Epistles of Paul to the Ephesians and to the Colossians* (*New International Commentary*; Grand Rapids, 1957).

Stott, J. R. W., *The Message of Ephesians* (*The Bible Speaks Today*; Leicester, 1979).

Swain, L., *Ephesians* (*New Testament Message*; Dublin, 1980).

Synge, F. C., *St. Paul's Epistle to the Ephesians* (London, 1941).

Thompson, G. H. P., *The Letters of Paul to the Ephesians, to the Colossians and to Philemon* (*New Cambridge Bible*; Cambridge, 1967).

Westcott, B. F., *St. Paul's Epistle to the Ephesians* (New York, 1906).

17

INTRODUCTION

I. THE NATURE AND TEACHING OF THE LETTER

As we begin to read the Letter to the Ephesians, we find that it opens in a way similar to the other New Testament letters that we recognize as Paul's: 'Paul, an apostle of Christ Jesus by the will of God, to the saints . . .'. As we continue, however, we find many features that make it stand out as different from the others. In the first place, apart from the fact that it speaks of Paul as privileged to be a minister of the gospel of the grace of Christ (3:2–13), and in consequence of his ministry imprisoned (3:1; 4:1; 6:20), and of Tychicus as the bearer of the letter (6:21–22), there are no other personal references, no greetings, no reminiscences, no messages to or from individuals such as have so large a place in the other letters which we know as Paul's. Furthermore, there are apparently no specific problems, either doctrinal or practical, that have given rise to this letter, and have to be dealt with in it, whereas all the other Pauline letters[1] are written to deal with particular issues and definite situations that we can assess from the letters themselves.

In many respects Ephesians reads more like a sermon – in some parts more like a prayer or a mighty doxology – than a letter written to meet some special need in a church or group of churches. It is like a sermon on the greatest and widest theme possible for a Christian sermon – the eternal purpose of God which he is fulfilling through his Son Jesus Christ, and working

---

[1]For the purposes of this Introduction, those letters which bear the name of Paul will be referred to as the Pauline letters.

out in and through the church. It is like a sermon, but the medium is the written word and the appeal is addressed to readers (3:4). This fact must stand against J. C. Kirby's suggestion[1] that the basis of Ephesians is liturgy, liturgy associated with Baptism, with Eucharist and with the Christian celebration of Pentecost. It seems wiser to say that the language of liturgy – of praise and prayer, related to the great central themes of Christian faith and worship – is used, but the form that we have is epistolary.[2] We have doxologies (1:3–14 and 3:20–21) and prayers (1:15–23 and 3:14–19), Old Testament quotations and at least one extract from an early Christian hymn (5:14), but in the setting of a letter with a specific, if widely scattered, readership.

One thought is allowed to lead on to another throughout the letter without constant reference to the situation of the readers. Chapters 1 – 3 are principally the doctrinal elaboration of the great theme, and chapters 4 – 6 teach what should be the practical consequences of it for human life and relationships. There is, however, no clear-cut division between doctrine and ethics, but rather an intimate linking of the two throughout.

After the initial address and greeting (1:1–2), there is praise of God which begins with God's eternal purpose for his people and continues in reference to adoption, redemption, revelation and reconciliation; and to the work of Father and Son is added that of the Spirit now and as assurance of the future (1:3–14). Thanksgiving, in particular for the readers of the letter, leads to prayer that they may have God-given wisdom to know the reality of their hope, the riches of their inheritance and the unlimited measure of the power available to them; and since that power is made known in Christ's resurrection and exaltation, the prayer closes with reference to what it means that Christ is 'head over all things for the church' (1:15–23). The next section (2:1–10) deals further with the meaning of redemption, life for those dead in sin, salvation by grace, a re-creation of human lives for the glory of God and as a demonstration of his great love. The further consequence is that since life and reconciliation are offered to all without distinction, the previously

---

[1] In *Ephesians, Baptism and Pentecost*.
[2] See van Roon, pp. 45–55; *cf.* Käsemann, pp. 288–297.

irremovable barrier that separated Jews and Gentiles is broken down. Both are brought into membership of the same body, built into the same living temple in which the Spirit of God dwells (2:11–22). Such thoughts lead naturally again to praise and prayer, but first the privilege of Paul's stewardship of the gospel is celebrated. In fresh terms the all-embracing purpose of God is described and in consequence it can be stressed that there is no need to lose heart in the face of suffering (3:1–13). The prayer then becomes a request for inner strength, for love, for the very 'fullness of God' (3:14–19) and praise that such a request can be made to one 'able to do far more abundantly than all that we ask or think' (3:20–21).

The exposition of such a majestic divine purpose leads on to the challenge 'to lead a life worthy of the calling', and this not just in individual terms. Humility and forbearance and love are required because there is a unity to be maintained (4:1–6). Yet in that unity there is diversity: all members have gifts for the building up of the body and for its growth even 'to the measure of the stature of the fullness of Christ' (4:7–16). There is obligation to put away all of the things that belonged to the former way of living, 'alienated from the life of God', and to 'put on the new nature' (4:17–24). Some of the things to be put away are detailed – dishonesty, anger, stealing, evil speaking, bitterness. In their place there must be integrity, generosity, the willingness to forgive, and, supremely, love, 'as Christ loved' (4:25 – 5:2). All impurity and self-seeking are to be laid aside, all the 'works of darkness' – to 'walk as children of light' means to follow 'all that is good and right and true' (5:3–14). Christian life involves doing 'the will of the Lord', being 'filled with the Spirit', and finds expression in songs of praise and in thankful hearts (5:15–20). Inter-personal relationships – people 'subject to one another out of reverence for Christ' (5:21) – are an essential part of that Christian living: husbands and wives (5:22–33), children and parents (6:1–4), slaves and masters (6:5–9). Finally it has to be realized that a spiritual warfare is involved – the principalities and powers of evil against the people of God who must stand firm and strong in the armour God supplies, with a constant dependence on God in prayer (6:11–20). Thus, with reference to Tychicus, the bearer of the letter, and with a final benediction, the letter closes (6:21–24).

II. DESTINATION

From the second century this letter was received almost univer-sally under the title 'to the Ephesians'. But there is evidence that the title is not truly original, and is, at least to some extent, a misnomer. The oldest manuscript of Ephesians that we possess, the Chester Beatty papyrus of about AD 200, and the great fourth-century codices Sinaiticus and Vaticanus, and certain other authorities do not have the words 'at Ephesus' in 1:1. Marcion in the mid-second century refers to this letter as the letter to the Laodiceans. This may have been because he had a copy with 'at Laodicea' inserted in 1:1 or, more probably, it was a deduction from the reference to the letter 'from Laodicea' in Colossians 4:16. At least there are no obvious doctrinal reasons why he should have said it was written to people other than the Ephesians if such was the original title. The evidence is com-plicated at this point in that the second-century Muratorian Fragment on the Canon refers to two letters, one to the Ephesians and one to the Laodiceans; but when we come to the third century we find the great biblical scholar Origen saying that the words 'at Ephesus' were not in the manuscripts that he knew. Tertullian, about the same time, accused the Marcionites of tampering with the title but he made no reference to the text. Basil and Jerome in the fourth century make it plain that the best manuscripts they had did not include the words.

If we could think of the letter without these words in 1:1 and without a title, we would have to admit that there is no clear evidence from the contents of the letter that it was sent to Ephesus, and a good deal that suggests that it could hardly have been addressed simply to the church in that city. For three years Paul had lived and worked in Ephesus (Acts 19 and 20:31). When in particular we consider the very moving way in which Paul addressed the elders of the church of Ephesus in Acts 20:18–35, we may well ask whether he could have written a letter to this church without reference to the time he spent there, without mention of any aspect of the situation in the church, and with no personal news of any kind. Instead the letter was written as if many, at least, of his readers were not well known to its author (1:15; 3:2; 4:20–21). The evidence of the nature of the letter as a whole strongly supports the textual evidence of 1:1 that this letter could hardly be a message written by the apostle Paul simply for his many friends and converts in the church of Ephesus.

Thus there are two questions that we must try to answer: To whom was the letter written? and, How did it come to be known as the letter of Paul to the Ephesians? Neither question can be answered with certainty, but there are a number of suggestions that have been made.

a. It was not sent to a particular church, but to any Christians who might read it. Some have argued that 1:1 makes sense without the words 'at Ephesus' or any similar place reference, reading 'the saints who are also faithful in Christ Jesus'. This is difficult grammatically;[1] 'faithful' is hardly an expression that, added to 'saints', requires such emphasis as is given by the article, participle and the linking 'and' together (*tois ousin kai*). The parallels in Romans, 1 and 2 Corinthians and Philippians point almost inevitably to the conclusion that there was originally a place-name in the verse. Moreover, there are passages that obviously were written with specific readers in mind, even if they were readers in a number of different churches (1:15ff.; 6:21–22).

b. It was sent to a particular church, but the address and personal greetings were later omitted so that the letter might have a more general use. It then happened to become attached particularly to Ephesus. The greatest difficulty about this suggestion is that in most of Paul's letters there are marks all the way through of the situation and the people to whom they were addressed. We could not remove the marks of the destination merely by removing the greetings and the address. This fact stands in particular against the view of Marcion that the letter was sent to Laodicea. It may be added that Colossians 4:16 speaks of a letter 'from Laodicea' and not simply 'to Laodicea', and indeed Paul would hardly have given greetings to particular Christians at Laodicea in Colossians 4:15 if he had been writing another letter to them at the same time.

---

[1]See, however, the commentary on 1:1, p. 52.

c. It was sent to a number of churches in a particular area, probably the Roman province of Asia. Internal and external evidence provides much to support this view. There are two forms of this suggestion. One copy of the letter, it is supposed, was taken round to the different churches, and a gap was left for the bearer to fill in the name as he went. Against this it has been argued that such an expedient cannot be paralleled in ancient letter-writing, but the answer can be given that 'so simple and common sense a plan does not require to be justified by precedents'.[1] Alternatively, it is suggested that there were a number of copies of the letter each bearing a different place-name. The copy addressed to Ephesus then became the letter accepted, because Ephesians was the most important church. If this were the case, however, it is strange that there is no trace of any other place-name in the manuscripts that have come down to us. The most cogent objection to the view that the letter was written to a group of churches in the Roman province of Asia is that we have several New Testament writings that were sent to a group of churches – 2 Corinthians, Galatians, 1 Peter, Revelation – but in each case the fact is made clear in their introductions. Why could not these churches of Asia have been addressed in such a way? We cannot give an answer to this question, except to say that the idea of a messenger putting in a different place-name as he reached each of the churches is not an impossible alternative as a manner of addressing them all.

d. Lastly, it has been argued by many in recent years that this strange uncertainty about the destination of the letters considered together with its other peculiar features, provides evidence in support of the hypothesis that Paul himself did not write Ephesians, but that it came from the hand of another after the apostle himself had died. To this issue of authorship we must now turn, and first of all consider the relation of Ephesians to certain other New Testament writings.

---

[1] E. Graham on 'Ephesians' in *A New Commentary on Holy Scripture*, edited by C. Gore, H. L. Goudge and A. Guillaume (London, 1928), pp. 538f.

III. EPHESIANS AND COLOSSIANS

Without fear of contradiction it may be said that there are more numerous and more sustained similarities between Ephesians and Colossians than between any other two New Testament letters. It is said that, with varying degrees of similarity, 75 of the 155 verses of Ephesians are found in Colossians. There are different categories in which the parallels between the two letters should be considered.

The plan and argument of the letters are similar. Both begin with a doctrinal section that shows forth the glory of Christ and the grandeur of his purpose; both proceed to apply this to personal life, and both move on to similar exhortations concerning human relationships. Within this framework there are whole sections that are very much alike. In the early part of the letters (1:15ff. and Col. 1:3ff.), in similar but by no means identical language, the writer gives thanks for the readers and prays for them; but admittedly this is a feature common to many of the Pauline letters. Of more significance is the way in which both deal with Christian living, speaking of putting off the old nature, and putting on the new (4:17ff. and Col. 3:5ff.). The 'walk' of the Christian is dealt with in both letters, the duty of thanksgiving, and its expression in praise and song (5:15–20 and Col. 3:16–17; 4:5–6). There is a close similarity in the instructions to husbands and wives, to parents and children, slaves and masters, though the Ephesians passage (5:22 – 6:9) is fuller than that in Colossians (3:18 – 4:1). In the writer's request for prayer for himself, there is in both cases a reference to his bonds, and to the mystery of the gospel to be made known (6:18–20 and Col. 4:3–4), and there is a similarity also in earlier references to the apostle's commission to make known the mystery of the gospel (3:1–13 and Col. 1:23–29). The parallels cannot be coincidental, but they are not such as one would find where a writer was dependent on another written record before him. They can only be explained by the assumption that the mind of the writer of Ephesians was full of the thought and expression of Colossians.

Furthermore, both in the sections already referred to, and also virtually throughout the two letters, there are many parallels in expression, parallels more numerous than we find between any other Pauline letters, parallels which demand an explanation in terms of some special connection between Ephesians and Colossians. It is impossible to deal with these parallels here, but a few examples can be taken.[1] In the following cases we have words or expressions that are not found in other Pauline letters, but are in both Ephesians and Colossians: the fullness of God or of Christ (1:23; 3:19; 4:13; Col. 1:19; 2:9); alienation from God or from his people (2:12; 4:18; Col. 1:21); redeeming the time (5:16; Col. 4:5); being rooted in Christ or in his love (3:17; Col. 2:7); redemption specifically interpreted as 'the forgiveness of sins' (1:7; Col. 1:14); the word of the truth of the gospel (1:13; Col. 1:5); forbearing one another (4:2; Col. 3:13); covetousness defined as idolatry (5:5; Col. 3:5); forgiving one another even as the Lord has forgiven (4:32; Col. 3:13); the joints of the body being knit together and the increase of the body in consequence (5:16; Col. 2:19); the giving of 'eye-service' as 'men-pleasers' (6:6; Col. 3:22). In respect of teaching it seems as if the great doctrinal statements of Colossians are assumed, and then there is built on them those doctrines which are the special emphasis of this letter. In Colossians we have a great exposition of the place of Christ in the universe; this is assumed in Ephesians but this letter goes further to show the cosmic significance of the church in fulfilling the great work of Christ. In Colossians there is emphasis on the reconciliation of men and women to God through the cross of Christ. In Ephesians, as we have seen, this is taken for granted, and we have the further truth of the reconciliation of people one to another through the cross in the body of Christ which is the fellowship of reconciliation.

Finally we must notice the references to Tychicus as bearer. In the parallel passages that we have noted in the two letters, there are hardly ever more than a few words in succession that are identical. The exception to this is the reference to Tychicus at the end of each letter. Here we have twenty-nine words in agreement between Ephesians and Colossians. This is the only strong case for literary dependence (6:21-22; Col. 4:7-8), and we seem forced to the conclusion that either the same writer wrote the

[1]For classification of the parallels see Mitton (*EE*) and Goodspeed (*KE*).

two together or else one writer for some special reason copied the words of the other.

This particular parallel needs further consideration, but apart from that we must say that the similarities between Colossians and Ephesians are such that they cannot be accounted for by saying that one is copied from the other. On the other hand, the parallels are so extensive and detailed that they cannot be explained as stemming from the common language of the early church, or even simply as coming from the mind of the same author. Whatever conclusions we may reach about the authorship, there is manifestly a special connection between the two letters. For a very long time it was accepted that the explanation of the features we have described was simply that Paul wrote the two letters at about the same time. He wrote the letter to the Colossians to meet a particular situation and danger in the church at Colossae. Then with his mind still working over the theme of the greatness and glory of Christ, but moving on to consider the place of the church in the purpose of God, he wrote Ephesians, this time without the limitation of any polemical aims. The greater measure of identity between 6:21–22 and Colossians 4:7–8 could be accounted for by the supposition that the apostle wrote the two conclusions together when both letters had been written and were about to be despatched. In the last hundred years, however, the Pauline authorship of Ephesians has been vigorously challenged, and it has been argued that the similarities (and differences) between Colossians and Ephesians are best accounted for by the view that Paul did not write Ephesians, but that someone else, whose mind was full of the thought and expression of Paul's letters, and especially of Colossians, wrote at a later date in his name and imitating his work. Even the virtual identity of 6:21–22 and Colossians 4:7–8 is explained in this way. J. L. Houlden puts it that 'such a crisis of authority' was 'facing the Church that desperate measures . . . were justified to keep it afloat; only the voice of Paul sufficed. Let it then ring out in tones as authentic as could be contrived.'[1]

The investigation of this view requires a more careful

---

[1]Houlden, p. 240.

consideration of the nature of the similarities between the letters than we have so far made. Opponents of Pauline authorship have pointed out, in particular, that although there is a great similarity in the words and phrases used, at times the same word or expression is used with a very different connotation. For example, although the same word 'mystery' is one of the key words of both letters, in Colossians (1:27) the 'mystery' is 'Christ in you, the hope of glory', in Ephesians it is that the Gentiles are fellow-heirs with the Jews (3:3, 6). In Colossians (1:20) reconciliation is between humanity and God, whereas in Ephesians it refers to the harmony of Jews and Gentiles in the one body of Christ (2:16). In Colossians (2:10) Christ is spoken of as the 'head [*kephalē*] of all rule and authority', while Ephesians (4:15) speaks of him as head of the church. (But here we should note that Colossians also speaks of him as head of the church, in 1:18.) Then there is the word *oikonomia*, a word used only once in the New Testament other than in Ephesians and Colossians; in Colossians 1:25 it is argued that it has the sense of stewardship, or an assignment given to a steward from God, but in Ephesians 1:10 and 3:2 it is rather a plan or arrangement of God that the word connotes. (It must be admitted, however, that the use in Ephesians 3:2 is very like that in Colossians.) Then we may compare the expression of Colossians 3:14, 'love, which is the bond of perfectness' (RV), with that of Ephesians 4:3, 'the bond of peace'.

Some have concluded that the same person could not have written both letters because differences of such a kind would not be found in the same writer. This very phenomenon of little differences and great similarities has, however, seemed to others most strongly to support the conclusion of Pauline authorship. Barry, for example, observing that 'the similarity is almost mingled with clear and characteristic difference, marking an independent coincidence' and that 'identical expressions occur again and again in entirely different contexts, and in different degrees of prominence', argues: 'These are exactly the phenomena we may expect when two letters are written at the same time to churches neither wholly identical nor wholly dissimilar in character, and under the guidance of distinct, yet complementary, ideas. They are wholly incompatible with dependence or deliberate copyism.' A more careful study of particular words and phrases than we can give here is necessary in order to make a fair judgment. Some of the expressions are studied from this point of view within their context in the Commentary proper (*e.g.* see on 3:4 for 'mystery'). We may only note here that in many cases the use of terms in the two letters differs in precisely the same way as we have found their doctrine to differ.

Mitton argues further, from his careful comparison of the two letters, that frequently one Ephesians passage corresponds to two passages in Colossians (*e.g.* 1:7 and Col. 1:14, 20; 1:15–16 and Col. 1:4, 9);[1] the reason for this he alleges to be that the later writer automatically linked in his mind two Colossians passages with which he was very familiar. Mitton's argument could fully be met only by an analysis as careful as his own. It does seem, however, that it could be countered by a number of examples where there are two Ephesians passages that correspond to one in Colossians (*e.g.* 3:7, 17 and Col. 1:23; 1:4, 2:16 and Col. 1:21–22; 1:10, 2:13–14 and Col. 1:20). At least there is no decisive argument concerning authorship here; but in justice to Mitton it must be said that he considers the matter alongside what he believes to be a similar phenomenon found when Ephesians is compared with other Pauline letters. To such a comparison we must now turn.

IV. EPHESIANS AND OTHER NEW TESTAMENT WRITINGS

a. *Other Pauline letters*

Comparison of Ephesians with other Pauline writings reveals certain features which have been taken as evidence against the Pauline authorship of the letter. Mitton, for example, finds three such features. In the first place he sees a conflation of the content of passages from other letters in Ephesians, as we have noted already in his argument about the relationship with Colossians. Nothing but an equally detailed argument could answer that of Mitton, but once again it is possible to find

[1]Mitton (*EE*), pp. 65–67.

examples where there might be said to be two Ephesians passages conflated in another letter.

A second argument of his in fact involves such a parallelism
between one passage of another Pauline letter and two or more
passages in Ephesians. Mitton feels that when we compare
Ephesians with other Pauline letters, we do not find the kind of
similarity we would expect if the same writer were drawing
upon his own mind, and therefore inevitably repeating some of
his earlier thoughts and expressions (*i.e.* we do not find the sort
of similarity that we do have between other Pauline letters); but,
rather, that certain great Pauline passages are uppermost in the
mind of the writer of Ephesians. There are sustained parallels, he says, to the 'purple passages' of Paul's writings; *cf.*
Romans 1:21–24 and Ephesians 4:17–19; Romans 3:20 – 4:2 and
Ephesians 1:7, 19, 2:5, 8; Romans 5:1–2 and Ephesians 2:17, 18,
3:11–12; Romans 8:9–39 and Ephesians 1:4–7, 11, 13–14, 21, 3:6,
16, 18–19; and he cites also other examples. We would not wish
to deny the existence of noteworthy parallels between
Ephesians passages and the 'purple passages' of Romans, 1 and
2 Corinthians, Galatians, Philippians and 1 Thessalonians.
Rather, in that Ephesians, unlike the other letters, does not deal
with particular problems, we would expect the letter's closest
parallels to be with the great doctrinal passages of those letters,
and this is the case. We would expect Ephesians to resemble
most closely those letters which have greater doctrinal sections
than the others (*e.g.* Romans and Colossians), and this is the
case. We would expect to find that Ephesians, if it were a letter
of pure Pauline doctrine and ethics without local references, had
a greater number of verses or expressions in common with other
Pauline letters than would one of the letters which abound in
local references. This again is undeniably the case.

A third argument that Mitton puts forward against Pauline
authorship is this fact that 88% of Ephesians is paralleled in the
other letters, whereas the percentage of convincing parallels
between any other letter and the rest is much lower. We cannot,
however, reach a conclusion simply from numbers. Subject-
matter and the varying length of the letters must be considered.
The fact that Paul writes his other letters with specific and
differing local problems and situations in mind automatically

reduces the likelihood of overlap in their vocabulary that we would expect. In the case of Ephesians, however, his main theme is the doctrinal and practical implications of the redeeming purpose of God in Christ, a theme upon which he bases his specific injunctions in the other letters and which for this reason makes reiteration of words and phrases found in other letters more likely.

A little more must be said about the argument that while the teaching of Ephesians emphasizes many of the same themes that we find in other Pauline letters, there are distinctive features presented in Ephesians, and in the view of some these argue strongly for different authorship.

One example, referred to briefly already, is the teaching of reconciliation through the cross of Christ. The work of the cross is shown to be for our redemption, for the forgiveness of our sins (1:7; 2:13, 16; *cf.* Rom. 5:6–10; 1 Cor. 15:3; Col. 1:14) that we might become the children of God and heirs of God's kingdom (1:5, 18; *cf.* Rom. 8:14–17; Gal. 3:26; 4:5–7). We have a clear, typically Pauline statement of the doctrine of justification by faith: 'by grace you have been saved through faith; and this is not your own doing, it is the gift of God – not because of works, lest any man should boast' (2:8–9; *cf.* Rom. 3:21–26; Gal. 2:16; 3:11, 24–25) – though to it is added emphatically the further purpose, 'we are his workmanship, created in Christ Jesus for good works, which God prepared beforehand, that we should walk in them' (2:10). Then, most important of all, after it has been stated that he has made peace by the blood of the cross, that those who were dead in sin might receive new life (2:1ff.; *cf.* Rom. 5:12–21; 6:21–23),[1] and have access to God (*cf.* Rom. 5:1–2), it is added that the cross is also the way of peace between one person and another, one group and another, the means of the breaking down of the middle wall of partition between Jew and Gentile, the instrument for killing the old enmity between them. So it can be said that because Christ came to bring peace, now 'through him we both have access in one Spirit to the Father' (2:18). This same emphasis on the cross as the means of unity in

---

[1] The contrast is also noted between this death in sin and new life through Christ, and the teaching of identification with Christ's death and resurrection as in Rom. 6:1ff.

the fellowship of the church is also seen in the way that this letter speaks of the apostolic privilege of the ministry of the gospel. We are accustomed to Paul's speaking of the privilege of preaching the gospel, and in particular of being called to evangelize the Gentiles (*e.g.* Rom. 1:13-16; 11:13; 15:15-20; Gal. 1:15-16; 2:9; Col. 1:24-29); but in this letter there is the further emphasis on the apostle's calling and privilege to communicate to others the 'mystery', the great revealed secret of the faith, that 'the Gentiles are fellow heirs, members of the same body' (3:6).

In teaching concerning the resurrection and exaltation of Christ we have the truth presented in a way that is familiar to us from Pauline letters (1:20-22; *cf.* Phil. 2:9-11; Col. 1:15-18). But here in Ephesians the climax of the statement of the exaltation of Christ is that God 'made him the head over all things for the church, which in his body, the fullness of him who fills all in all' (1:22-23). It is the purpose of God that people who were dead in trespasses and sins should be raised up together with Christ (*cf.* Rom. 6:3-11; Col. 2:12; 3:1-3), and with Christ be made to sit in the heavenly places (Eph. 2:5-6); but the treatment of the resurrection and exaltation in this letter goes further than this. He has 'ascended far above all the heavens, that he might fill all things', and that he might so give gifts to his church that it might grow 'to the measure of the stature of the fullness of Christ' (4:9-16).

We have also typically Pauline teaching about the Holy Spirit. It is by the Spirit that God indwells those who believe in Christ (2:22; 3:16-17; 5:18; *cf.* Rom. 8:9-11; 1 Cor. 3:16; 6:19); the Spirit is the 'seal' and 'guarantee' given them by God (1:13-14; 4:30; *cf.* Rom. 8:23; 2 Cor. 1:22; 5:5). He helps them in prayer (6:18; *cf.* Rom. 8:26-27), and is the means not only of access to God (2:18) but of wisdom in the things of God and enlightenment in the practical details of life (1:9, 17; 3:5; *cf.* 1 Cor. 2:10-13). Again, however, the teaching of the work of the Spirit finds its greatest development in connection with the church and its unity. The church needs gifts for its growth (4:7ff.; *cf.* 1 Cor. 12:4-11) and the goal of the use of these gifts in their diversity is 'the unity of the faith', the development of the church in all its members 'to mature manhood'.

What has been said already about other doctrines is sufficient indication of the great place that the doctrine of the church has in this letter. But the difference between this and other Pauline letters would seem to be one of emphasis and of degree rather than of essential teaching. There is little or nothing here that is new, but we have a greater emphasis on the universal church and its unity, and a greater variety of ways of expressing the purpose of the church than we have in any other Pauline letter. The writer's mind is manifestly filled with the sense of the mighty purpose of God for his church. He speaks, as we have seen, of the exaltation of Christ, and the climax of it all is his headship of the church which is his body (1:22–23; *cf.* 1 Cor. 12:27; Col. 1:18, 24; 2:19). He speaks of the reconciliation of people not only to God but to one another, and emphasizes that this is in the church, 'the household of God' (2:19; *cf.* Gal. 6:10), the temple built on the foundation of the apostles and prophets (2:20–21; *cf.* 1 Cor. 3:16; 2 Cor. 6:16) that is God's habitation in the Spirit. We have noted what the writer says in Ephesians 4 about the church and Christian unity. He goes on to deal with the very different subject of Christian marriage, taking as an illustration the Old Testament figure of the people of God as the bride (*cf.* 2 Cor. 11:2), and thereby expresses great truths about the relationship of the Lord to his church. Finally we should note the cosmic significance that he gives to the church. It has a great divine purpose in the world, to proclaim Christ and bring people into unity in him; but it has an eternal purpose, a task which is not complete in this world and in this age – to make known 'to the principalities and powers in the heavenly places' what is 'the manifold wisdom of God' (3:10–11).

It is thus fair to say that the doctrine of this letter is essentially Pauline, but developed along such lines as are necessary in the task of expounding the great theme of the whole letter, and with the polemical requirements so relevant in other letters removed. Arguments against Pauline authorship on the basis of a comparison of the teaching of Ephesians and that of other Pauline letters cannot therefore be regarded as at all conclusive.

We must turn now to the comparison of our letter with other New Testament writings, and in each case try to see if there is any evidence of direct literary dependence, or if in other ways we can find features that give indication of the probable date of the writing of Ephesians.

b. 1 Peter

There are some important parallels between 1 Peter and Ephesians. The opening doxologies are similar (but that of 2 Corinthians 1:3ff. is not dissimilar); and the treatments of the relations of husbands and wives, masters and slaves are alike (5:22–23; 6:5–9; 1 Pet. 2:18 – 3:7) but the parallel in this case is not as close as that between 1 Peter and Colossians. There are also parallels in what is said of the exaltation of Christ and the subjection to him of all powers (1:20–21; 1 Pet. 3:22); in references to the Christian warfare (6:10–18; 1 Pet. 5:8–9), to the gospel as hidden before but now made clear, and to its communication to angels (3:5–6, 10; 1 Pet. 1:10–12), to the purpose of God before the foundation of the world (1:4; 1 Pet. 1:19–20), to the lusts of the flesh and the children of obedience and disobedience (2:2–3; 1 Pet. 1:14; 2:11), to putting away guile and evil speaking (4:25, 31; 1 Pet. 2:1), and to the people of God's own possessions (1:14; 1 Pet. 2:9). We have the word *eusplanchnoi* for 'tenderhearted' used in the New Testament only in 4:32 and 1 Peter 3:8. Many of the likenesses are sufficiently accounted for by the general similarity of the language used by different writers in the early church to speak of Christian teaching and conduct. An even more satisfactory explanation of the close parallels is given in the theory of Archbishop Carrington, developed by Selwyn, that there were certain standard forms that the catechetical teaching of the church was taking even at this early stage.[1] If there is often a closer resemblance between 1 Peter and Ephesians than between 1 Peter and Colossians, the reason could well be that in Colossians there is of necessity an adaptation of the catechetical teaching to a particular situation, whereas in Ephesians this is not necessary. Various theories of literary dependence, of Ephesians on 1 Peter or vice versa, have

---

[1] P. Carrington, *The Primitive Christian Catechism* (Cambridge, 1940) and E. G. Selwyn, *The First Epistle of St. Peter* (London, 1949), pp. 363ff.

been put forward, but it is hard to argue at all conclusively for such dependence, as the inability of the exponents of these theories to agree on the direction of the borrowing evidently shows.

c. Luke and Acts

Similarities have also been pointed out between Ephesians and Luke and Acts. There is in Ephesians (1:20; 4:8–10) the same emphasis on the ascension and exaltation of Christ that we find in Luke and Acts (see Lk. 24:51; Acts 1:9; and Acts 2:32–36; 7:55), but we also find this in other Pauline letters, and in any case it is a matter of basic doctrine. The references to the 'purpose' of God (1:5; Lk. 2:14), to the goal of the work of Christ as holiness and righteousness (4:24; Lk. 1:75), to the contrast between light and darkness (5:8–13; Lk. 11:33–36; Acts 26:18), to the girding of the loins (6:14; Lk. 12:35), have all been taken as arguments for literary dependence, but their use in the early church must have been more general than would allow us to argue for literary dependence from this slight evidence. For this same reason no argument can be based on the fact that the expression 'filled with the Spirit' (5:18), so common in the Lucan writings, is found in Ephesians only of the Pauline letters. Much has been made of the close similarities between Ephesians and the address to the Ephesian elders in Acts 20, *e.g.* the reference to the 'counsel' (*boulē*) of God, to lowliness, to the ministry of the grace of God. But if Ephesians is the work of the apostle, and Luke gave a substantially accurate account of Paul's address to the Ephesian elders, this is what we would expect; and this explanation is at least as likely as the theory that a later writer made use of what had already been written by Luke in Acts 20. Rather than suggesting literary dependence, the parallels tend to give a ring of truth to both.

One writer, R. P. Martin, has taken the comparison of Luke-Acts and Ephesians further.[1] Finding linguistic parallels, the development of similar themes, and a similar background situation ('gnosticizing and antinomian tendencies' in the Gentile

---

[1] 'An Epistle in search of a Life-setting' in *ExpT* 79 (1968), pp. 296ff.

churches of Asia Minor and Gentile Christians boasting an independence of Israel), he has argued for a common authorship. His arguments are hardly convincing, though undoubtedly similarities exist.

d. The Johannine literature

The Johannine literature must also be considered briefly, as it has been said that in Ephesians we have Pauline teaching and expression influenced also by Johannine theology and terminology. Moffatt says that the writer of Ephesians was breathing the atmosphere in which the Johannine literature took shape. It is true that there is a stronger emphasis on realized eschatology than in other Pauline letters. There is a common use of some of the Johannine keywords, 'light' and 'darkness', 'life' and 'death', 'love', 'knowledge, etc. There is an emphasis on the unity of the church in Ephesians which is more like John 17 than anything in the other Pauline letters. There is frequent reference to Christians finding their life 'in Christ' (cf. Jn. 15:1–7), to Christ's indwelling his church (3:17; Jn. 14:20; 15:4–7) and cleansing and sanctifying it (5:26; Jn. 15:3; 17:17, 19; 1 Jn. 1:7), to the descent and ascent of Christ (4:9; Jn. 3:13, 31; 7:39), to Jesus as beloved of the Father (1:6; Jn. 3:35; 10:17; 15:9; 17:23–26). Once again, however, literary dependence cannot be argued. The question of date may be raised (see below on this), but nearly all of the parallels mentioned involve expressions whose use can be illustrated from Christian writings earlier than the commonly accepted date of the Johannine literature.

There are also particular parallels noted between Ephesians and Revelation, as well as those of the kind just mentioned. There is reference to the apostles and prophets as foundations of the church (2:20; 3:5; Rev. 10:7; 18:20; 21:14), to refusing to have fellowship with evil (5:11; Rev. 18:4), to the church as the bride of Christ (5:25–33; Rev. 19:7; 21:2, 9; 22:17), to sitting in heavenly places with Christ (2:6; Rev. 3:21), to the symbol of the seal (1:13; 4:30; Rev. 7:2–3). In none of these cases, however, is the language and thought peculiar to Ephesians and Revelation, nor can they be taken to support any argument on the dating of Ephesians.

e. Hebrews

A comparision of Ephesians and Hebrews reveals certain similar doctrines stressed in both: atonement through the death of Christ, the cleansing of the church, the exaltation of Christ, and our access to the Father through him; but we can hardly base any argument for authorship or date on this.

That there are marked parallels between Ephesians and these non-Pauline writings cannot be denied. Two things, however, need to be said. A good number, at least, of the parallels listed are common also to other Pauline letters and these writings. Then also the fact that Ephesians has more New Testament parallels than the other letters can be explained adequately by the fact that Ephesians is not a controversial writing, and we would naturally expect more overlap where the common Christian vocabulary used in preaching and teaching is involved than where particular problems are treated. This letter, if Paul's, is, moreover, one of his latest and most mature works, and it could fairly readily be established in argument that there are greater similarities between the non-Pauline writings considered above and the later Pauline letters, than between them and Paul's earlier letters. We may well ask whether the similarities between Ephesians and these various writings are not simply eloquent testimony to the great and increasing measure of similarity in the early Christian preaching and teaching, whether in Asia, Rome, Ephesians or Antioch, whether from the lips of Peter, Paul, John or any other. Nowhere are the similarities such as to make direct dependence (as there manifestly is between 2 Peter and Jude) a necessary deduction, nor yet such as to make some special connection (as between Ephesians and Colossians) appear inevitable.

V. ARGUMENTS FOR A LATER DATE

Apart from the question of the similarity of Ephesians to other New Testament writings, it is argued that there are signs in the letter itself which indicate that it was written at a date later than Paul's death.

It has been argued, in particular, that Paul spent most of his life striving for the equality of Jews and Gentiles in the church. Could he have written, as appears the case in Ephesians, as if this controversy was settled, and required no further argument? But for Paul it *was* settled, as his argument in Romans (with the polemic of Galatians removed) itself shows. It is true that the presentation in Romans 9 – 11 of the place of Jews and Gentiles in the purpose of God is different from the presentation in Ephesians. There is not elsewhere the particular argument that it was the object of the work of Christ in his cross to bring Jews and Gentiles into one, but that could well have been a natural result of his further meditation on the work of Christ and the unity of the church. The task of the church in working out the purpose of God is basic to this letter, and this accounts for the way in which the question of Jews and Gentiles is treated. Justification by faith is not the primary argument, as in Romans and Galatians; therefore here the meaning of the death of Christ can be related most prominently to the realization of peace both between humanity and God and between one person and another. The reasons for the past division between Jew and Gentile are not vital in the way that they were at the time of the writing of Galatians, and so the realization of the union of the two can be treated as an illustration (indeed to Paul the most noteworthy illustration) of the unity that Christ brings. Findlay argues strongly that it would be hard for anyone other than the apostle Paul to have written of Jews and Gentiles in just the way in which chapter 2 of this letter is written.[1] He saw them from the position of one who had been a strict Jew, who had looked at Gentiles across 'the dividing wall of hostility' (2:14), and who had then been converted to Christ and become the apostle to the Gentiles.

A little more must be said about the teaching on the unity of the church. It is argued that the concept of Ephesians is here more akin to that of Ignatius than to the position with which we are familiar from Paul's letters, where it is usually only the unity of the local church that is considered. It is said that this letter

[1]Findlay, pp. 5f.

must date from the time when sects began to appear and abound. It is true that the author in Ephesians develops concepts of the nature and function of the church that are in advance of anything in other Pauline letters (*e.g.* in 2:20–22; 3:10, 21; 5:23–32), but in the other letters we do find a view of the church universal, not just the local church, and indeed a regard for the functions of the church reaching beyond this world (*e.g.* see 1 Cor. 4:9; 12:28; 15:9; Gal. 1:13; Phil. 3:6). We should expect development and increasing understanding in a man with as virile and receptive a mind as Paul's; and if he had just been dealing with the cosmic significance of Christ in Colossians, it is not surprising that he should go on to deal in another letter with the cosmic place of the church. There is, moreover, a great difference between the thought of Ephesians and that of the Ignatian letters in the matter of church unity. In the former the whole emphasis is on spiritual unity without reference to organization, while in the latter it is on unity under a single leader, the bishop.

One other particular argument should be considered at this point. It is asked: Would an apostle speak as the writer of this letter does in 3:5 of 'holy apostles and prophets' (*cf.* 'apostles and prophets' in 2:20) as those to whom the message is revealed, and as the foundation of the church? Mitton says that the emphasis on their authority 'is reminiscent of the campaign for the proper recognition of duly authorised leaders which took place in the generation after Paul'.[1] Yet in 1 Corinthians 3:10 and 9:2 Paul spoke of the apostles as the first builders on the foundation of Jesus Christ and such building work was the sign and seal of the genuineness of an apostle. Paul realized the priority of the position of the apostles (1 Cor. 12:28), and without pride he felt the dignity and responsibility of his own place amongst them (1 Cor. 9:1; Gal. 1:11–17; 2:6–9); and certainly in Ephesians there is no undue stress on apostolic authority. It hardly needs to be added that the New Testament use of the word 'holy' did not involve the connotation of special sanctity of life, but rather the emphasis on the calling to dedication of life (see on 1:1).

[1]Mitton (*EE*), p. 19.

There are in fact, on the other hand, even more cogent arguments for placing this letter not long, if at all, after the lifetime of Paul. It was in use very early. Probably Clement of Rome in the year 95 knew it. Hippolytus says that Basilides, the Ophites and the Valentinians used it, and they are among the earliest of Gnostic sects. The evidence of the early use of the letter is something which those who doubt its Pauline authorship find difficult to explain. There is no reference in it to the persecution of Christianity, which would be strange indeed if it was first written for the churches of the Roman Province of Asia about the time when the Apocalypse was written, or even somewhat earlier. There is, moreover, no reference to the heresies which became widespread in Asia not very long after the death of Paul. These things at least point strongly to the conclusion that if Ephesians was not written by Paul it must have been written not long after his death.

We must now turn to considerations that help us more directly to determine whether the letter itself is such as would have been more likely to come from the apostle than from another person writing in his name.

VI. OTHER EVIDENCE FOR AUTHORSHIP

We noted at the very beginning of this Introduction that Ephesians is different in form from any other letter that we regard as Paul's. It is said with a real measure of truth that it is hardly a letter, but more a written sermon or homily. It is asked whether even a 'circular letter' written for a number of churches, as is Galatians, would have been written as impersonally as this is.

It is also argued further that such personal references as there are do not ring true. Would Paul have said to Christians to whom he wrote, 'assuming that you have heard of the stewardship of God's grace that was given to me' (3:2)? It is true that there is an element of doubt such as Paul could hardly have expressed to the Ephesian church, but it is not unthinkable that Paul should speak in this way, and then say, 'When you read this you can perceive my insight into the mystery of Christ' (see

3:4), especially if he realized that he was writing to Christians over a wide area, some of whom would know him well, but others little more than his name and apostleship.

Then 3:8 raises a difficulty for some, when Paul speaks of himself as 'the very least of all the saints'. The words have been spoken of as an exaggerated imitation of 1 Corinthians 15:8–9, 'a mild and passionless echo of the amazed sense of personal unworthiness of grace which is expressed in the Corinthian verses' (Allan). Others find in these words one of the clearest marks of the letter's genuineness. Abbott comments that the expression does not derive from 'calculated imitation; it has the stamp of a spontaneous outflow of an intense feeling of unworthiness'. Bruce (*EE*) says, 'No disciple of Paul's would have dreamed of giving the apostle so low a place.' At least it is difficult to think of an imitator at one moment trying to show the greatness of Paul's understanding and statement of the gospel, as many regard 3:2–4, and the next moment giving him such a humble place.

That there is a difference in style between this and other Pauline letters is undoubted. The style here is more diffuse. There is no closely worked out argument. The doctrinal passages are lyrical rather than argumentative. There are long sentences, full of participles, synonymous expressions, epexegetic genitives (*e.g.* 1:3–14, 15–23; 2:1–9; 3:1–7). Yet if we have to compare the style with that of Colossians, we would not deem that of Colossians greater and more worthy, nor would we say that the difference is such as to make identity of authorship impossible. Differences could surely be explained on the basis of the difference of purpose between the two letters, and the inevitable difference between writing a letter to meet a particular need and the attempt to set down on paper the result of a deep and fruitful meditation on the central themes of the gospel. In Ephesians there was no need for argument to meet objections and difficulties; we have rather what Dodd calls 'a prophetic declaration of incontrovertible patent facts, in a new and lofty setting of eternal principles'.[1] The writer here 'does not argue, he makes dogmatic statements';[2] so he has scope for waxing

---

[1]Dodd, p. 1222.   [2]Lock, p. 11.

lyrical. We may add that when Colossians (as in 1:12–22) and Romans (as in 1:1–6 and 8:32–39) do the same, their style approaches most nearly to that of Ephesians.

Analysis of the vocabulary of Ephesians reveals that the letter has forty-two words not used elsewhere in the New Testament. This figure is not great when compared with those for other Pauline letters.[1] It would seem more significant that thirty-eight words are used elsewhere in the New Testament but not in other Pauline letters. But such arguments from vocabulary are precarious. It is necessary to study the subject-matter of the passages in which the words are found. For example, in Ephesians quite a number of the *hapax legomena* belong to such particular descriptions as that of the Christian armour. Some of the words listed as found in the New Testament but not elsewhere in Paul are not really peculiar to this letter in that words with the same stem are found in others. Some, again, are common words that Paul or any other first-century writer might well have used.

Particular words merit special consideration, but this cannot be done in detail here. A few examples may be taken. It is noted that *diabolos* is used here and in the Pastorals, while the other Pauline letters use *Satanas*. Acts and John use the two indifferently, however, and there seems no reason why Paul should not have used *diabolos*. There are phrases such as 'in the heavenly places', 'the Father of glory', 'before the foundation of the world', which are said to be non-Pauline. Others mention as words that are not Pauline, *kosmokratōr* of 6:12 ('world ruler'), *sōtērion* for 'salvation', *methodeia* for the 'wiles' of the devil. But we should not be surprised to find in such a letter as this, if it is Paul's, words not found in other letters, words more familiar to us from other strands of early Christian thought. The apostle's mind was fertile and open to influence from the phraseology of his opponents and so surely from the terminology of other Christians. More important is the argument which we have considered already, that certain key words like *mustērion* and *oikonomia* are used in Ephesians in a way that is different from their use in other Pauline letters. But in this case, as with

---

[1] For details of this comparison, see Abbott, p. 15.

vocabulary generally, an imitator would try to follow closely the Pauline usage, and the differences are as hard or harder to explain on the theory that another wrote Ephesians in the name of the apostle.

We have considered the special development of doctrine that we find in Ephesians, and we have compared the teaching of the letter with that of Colossians. There are certain other arguments that have been used in the attempt to show that the letter includes doctrine and subject-matter that could hardly have come from the pen of the apostle. It is urged that in Ephesians a number of divine acts are ascribed to Christ that in other letters are ascribed to the Father – *e.g.* the work of reconciliation (2:16; *cf.* Col. 1:20; 2:13–14); the appointment of apostles, prophets, *etc.* (4:11; *cf.* 1 Cor. 12:28). But there are examples of the reverse proceeding. In 4:32 it is said that 'God in Christ forgave you' (*cf.* Col. 3:13). Both ways of speaking of the works of God can be found in a number of Pauline letters. To the apostle, what is the work of the Father is the work of the Son. Since he could say, 'for us there is one God, the Father, from whom are all things and for whom we exist, and one Lord, Jesus Christ, through whom are all things and through whom we exist' (1 Cor. 8:6), there can be no validity in this kind of argument. What God does, he does through Christ (2 Cor. 5:18–19); and what Christ does, he does according to the will of the Father.

To some, a more important argument is that the eschatology of Ephesians is realized rather than futurist as it is in Paul's earlier letters, and even in Philippians. It is sometimes said that 2:7 and 3:21 envisage a long time before the end. In the Commentary we must consider whether this is a true interpretation of the actual passages. The eschatology of Colossians and Ephesians is certainly not unlike. That there is a change of emphasis from Paul's earlier letters is undoubtedly true; but the hope of the parousia is not lost. The Holy Spirit is the guarantee of the future inheritance, for the experience of salvation is not yet complete in the Christian's life here and now (1:13–14; 4:30). The church will one day in the future be presented spotless to Christ (5:27). There will be a future day of reckoning when all will have to stand before God as judge (5:6; 6:8). If a strong case could be made for there being a real difference between the eschatology of Colossians and Ephesians, that might have bearing on the question of authorship, but such a case cannot be made.

We have considered the way in which this letter deals with the matter of the relationship between Jews and Gentiles. Independently of this issue it is said that the Jews are treated in Ephesians in a way that Paul himself could never have treated them. In 2:3 they are said to be guilty of the same immoralities as the Gentiles, while in 2:11–12 there is what has been called a scornful reference to circumcision. It may be asked, however, whether Paul says less about the sins of the Jews, even sins of the flesh, in Romans 2:21–24, and whether he speaks there any less severely than this letter does. Moreover, nothing more derogatory to circumcision is said in Ephesians than in Romans 2:25–29, Philippians 3:2–3, and Colossians 2:11; in fact the spirit of the four passages is very similar. (See further on 2:11–12.)

VII. THE WORK OF AN IMITATOR OR OF THE APOSTLE?

We must say, with Mitton, that no single argument for or against Pauline authorship of Ephesians can be described as conclusive. It is the cumulative strength of all the arguments that must be considered. However, the earliest writers who cast doubt on the authenticity of the letter were content with negative arguments. More recently an attempt has been made, notably by Goodspeed (*ME*) and Mitton (*EE*), to suggest a situation after the time of Paul's death for which they believe that this letter was written.

Goodspeed's theory is that some years after the time of their being written, Paul's letters, written mostly to individual churches, were largely neglected or forgotten. A few people valued and kept them, and there were some who specially reverenced him for his letter to the church at Colossae, perhaps members of that church who were at first acquainted with that letter only. One man in particular knew and loved this letter. After Acts was published – Goodspeed puts that at about the year 85 – and Paul was seen to stand out in all his greatness for his apostolic labours, this man decided to find as many as he could of Paul's letters. He collected them, read and re-read them, filled his mind with them, but most of all with Colossians which he knew first and loved most. Then he decided to republish them with an introduction that would lift the message of Paul above the topical issues of other days and would be simply a restatement of his understanding of the eternal truth of God in Christ. He did not want to obtrude his own personality, and so he wrote in Paul's name, and longed that the message of Paul might be heard again through him. Goodspeed says that this fact accounts for Ephesians being a 'mosaic of Pauline materials', 'almost a Pauline anthology'. The close similarity to Colossians is thus accounted for; the difficulties that have been felt about Pauline authorship are resolved. Goodspeed even goes so far as to guess that Onesimus was the author.[1] His views have won much support, especially in America.

The English scholar Mitton adopted the essentials of Goodspeed's theory, and believed that the relationship of Ephesians to the other Pauline letters and to Colossians in particular could be explained in some such way. The dependence was thus not a literary dependence; the writing was done by one whose mind was filled with Paul's letters. Only at the end, in the reference to Tychicus, did he refer to his copy.

J. C. Kirby has a different theory.[2] As Paul's letters began to be circulated, 'a request came to Ephesus for a copy of their letter or letters from Paul'. One of the leaders there presented in response 'a distillation of the thought of the apostle'. This was derived largely from 'the worshipping tradition' of a church where the apostle had spent three years. Kirby adds at this point his idea of the special dependence on a liturgy for Pentecost that the writer allowed to form 'the basis of his letter'.

There remain many problems associated with theories such as those of Goodspeed, Mitton and Kirby. The first is the strong external evidence of Pauline authorship, and the very early use of the letter which we have noted above. There is never any doubt expressed about its authenticity in the early church. There

---

[1] A modification of this view is suggested by G. H. P. Thompson (New Cambridge Bible) to the effect that Paul left Tychicus to put together his teaching as presented in this letter.

[2] Kirby, pp. 165–172.

is certainly no textual support for Ephesians being put at the head of the Pauline corpus, as if to introduce the other letters.

Then it can truly be said that there are features that are so typically Pauline that we would hardly expect to find them in an imitator. There is the characteristically Pauline way of connecting together doctrinal truth and moral duty. There is the Pauline habit of breaking off at a word to deal with a new subject (3:1–14; *cf.* Rom. 5:13ff.; Phil. 3:1ff.). We cannot ultimately argue from the similarity or the differences in vocabulary and phraseology – as we have seen, the argument can be taken either way. But in this letter we have the unrestrained praise of the glory of Christ, the uninhibited declaration of the wonder of his purpose for his church, not in the measured terms of one who writes under a sense of obligation to follow faithfully his great predecessor, but under the free inspiration of the Spirit.

However differently pseudonymity may have been regarded in the ancient world from the way that we would regard it, we find in this letter such a combination of authority and humility, and such an expression of privilege and responsibility (both Pauline traits), as would be very hard to imitate effectively. Any imitator is betrayed by his inferiority, but, as Scott says, this letter 'contains nothing which might not have been written by Paul, while it is everywhere marked by a grandeur and originality of thought which would seem utterly beyond the reach of a mere imitator'.[1] Could an imitator have produced a work so like those of the apostle, and yet written with such freedom and originality? Käsemann's picture of 'craftsmanship which united innumerable pieces of thoroughly disparate origin'[2] does not seem a satisfactory description of the document we have. Similarly the explanations of Goodspeed and Mitton are not adequate. It is possible, though unlikely, that there was a person of such spiritual calibre – otherwise unknown to us – in the generation after Paul's death, as could write like this. Yet the fact remains that the greatness of such an author and his dependence on Colossians (and other Pauline writings) are hard to put together. As Dodd puts it, 'Do we find such faithful dependence and such daring originality in

[1]Scott, p. 136.   [2]Käsemann, p. 288.

one and the same person?'[1]

That there is point in many of the difficulties that have been raised concerning the authenticity of Ephesians cannot be denied. The special features of the letter when set alongside other Pauline letters demand explanation. But we would still ask whether the difficulties are lessened at all by positing an imitator. It seems that by far the most likely solution is still the traditional one. We suppose therefore that Paul wrote Colossians from his confinement in Rome to meet special difficulties and dangers in the church at Colossae. Then, as he thought over and expressed the truth of the person of Christ, he was led on in his meditation to dwell on God's purpose in Christ as it is to be worked out in the church. He thought not just of Colossae, but of all the churches, especially those of the Roman province of Asia. He saw how they needed to be given a vision of the greatness of their calling and of the importance of the life and unity of the church as the body of Christ. So, shortly after writing Colossians, he wrote Ephesians. Colossians 4:15–16 refers to a letter not written to Laodicea, but which would reach Colossae 'from Laodicea'. In other words it seems that this letter, which he speaks of as written at the same time as Colossians, was in the nature of a circular letter. We believe that it is very probable, therefore, that the letter before us is the one to which Colossians 4:15–16 refers. The likelihood is increased if we consider that as the church of Colossae saw fit to preserve the little letter to Philemon, they would surely be anxious to preserve this general letter sent to the churches of the area.

Thus we imagine Colossians written, then Ephesians. Then the apostle penned the conclusion to Colossians, and immediately turned from writing that to address his closing personal message to the wider group of churches: 'that you also may know how I am . . . Tychicus . . . will tell you everything'. So Tychicus went off as bearer of the two letters and also of the personal letter to Philemon. He would have received explicit instructions concerning the churches of Asia to which he should take it. No one name was put in the address of our letter; the messenger could put in the relevant name at each place. In the

[1]Dodd, p. 1225.

years that followed several of the churches might have been found in possession of a copy. Perhaps only that in Ephesus had a name in it, and as Ephesus was the most famous church the letter would be copied most frequently from there, and so come to be named as we have it, 'The letter of Paul to the Ephesians'.

ANALYSIS

I. INTRODUCTION (1:1–23)
   a. *Greeting* (1:1–2)
   b. *Praise for God's purpose and blessings in Christ* (1:3–14)
   c. *Prayer for divine enlightenment* (1:15–23)

II. LIFE IN CHRIST (2:1 – 3:21)
   a. *New life from the dead* (2:1–10)
   b. *The reconciliation of Jews and Gentiles* (2:11–22)
   c. *The privilege of proclamation* (3:1–13)
   d. *Renewed prayer* (3:14–21)

III. UNITY IN THE BODY OF CHRIST (4:1–16)
   a. *Maintaining the unity* (4:1–6)
   b. *Diversity in unity* (4:7–16)

IV. PERSONAL STANDARDS (4:17 – 5:21)
   a. *New life to replace the old* (4:17–24)
   b. *Truth and love to replace falsehood and bitterness*
      (4:25 – 5:2)
   c. *Light to replace the darkness* (5:3–14)
   d. *Wisdom to replace folly* (5:15–21)

V. RELATIONSHIPS (5:22 – 6:9)
   a. *Husbands and wives* (5:22–33)
   b. *Children and parents* (6:1–4)
   c. *Servants and masters* (6:5–9)

VI. CONCLUSION (6:10–24)
    a. The Christian conflict (6:10–20)
    b. Final message and greeting (6:21–24)

COMMENTARY

I. INTRODUCTION (1:1–23)

A. GREETING (1:1–2)

1. All Paul's letters begin in a similar way. Following the style of the letter-writing of the day, he mentions first the writer, then the readers, and then comes the greeting. But the conventional manner of the time is lifted to a higher level. Writer and readers are described from the standpoint of their relationship to God in Christ; and the conventional greeting has become a Christian benediction.

Apostle is the title Paul most frequently gives himself. As meaning basically 'one sent', it speaks of the great privilege, but also of the divine compulsion, of the commission laid upon him. He could not think of himself in his relationship to others except in terms of his being sent to all with the gospel (*cf.* 2 Cor. 5:16). He is what he is *by the will of God*; and this is no mere permission, as the use of the same word in verses 5, 9 and 11 makes clear. It is God's positive purpose that makes Paul a man under authority, and enables him to write with authority. He is always at pains to stress that his calling is due to no personal merit (*cf.* 1 Cor. 15:9; Gal. 1:13–15; 1 Tim. 1:12–16); his authority is not self-assumed. Both are entirely of God (*cf.* especially Gal. 1:1); and on that fact he relies, especially when his mission is challenged.

The frequent New Testament designation of Christians as *saints* is the first of a number of words in chapter 1 whose meaning can be understood fully only by a consideration of their

Old Testament background. The saints are the holy ones, *hagioi*. In Old Testament days the tabernacle, the temple, the sabbath, and the people themselves were holy as they were consecrated, or set apart, for the service of God. People are not 'saints' in this sense by personal merit; they are set apart by God, and in consequence they are called to live in holiness. Thus the word expresses at once the privilege and the responsibility of the calling of every Christian, not the attainment of a select few. As we have seen in the Introduction when considering the destination of the letter, the words *at Ephesus* are absent from some of the best MSS, and yet grammar almost certainly requires a place-name in the original.[1] So we have concluded that it is likely that Ephesus was only one of a number of places to which this letter was sent.

The faithful (*pistoi*), a term often used for Christians in the New Testament, may mean those who have faith, or those who show fidelity. Here both ideas may be included; they are believers and their calling is to faithfulness. They are those who believe in the Lord, but the phrase *in Christ Jesus* means much more than alluding to the object of their faith. The phrase, so frequently used by Paul, especially in this letter, sums up very much of his understanding of the gospel. It, or an equivalent, is used eleven times in verses 1–14 alone. Christians not only have faith in him; their life is in him. As the root in the soil, the branch in the vine (*cf.* Jn. 15:1ff.), the fish in the sea, the bird in the air, so the place of the Christian's life is in Christ. Physically his or her life is in the world; spiritually it is lifted above the world to be in Christ (*cf.* Col. 3:1–3). We have a pointed juxtaposition of two phrases as Paul addresses his readers in Colossians 1:2 as 'in Christ' and 'in Colossae'. There is the implication that wherever Christians may be, in whatever difficult environment, threatened by materialism or paganism, in danger of being engulfed by the power of the state or overwhelmed by the pressures of non-Christian life, they are *in Christ*. This is not mysticism, but is intended to express the very practical truth that Christians, if faithful to their calling, will not try to be self-sufficient, or to

---

[1] It is just possible to take it as Caird does, the *hagioi* originally including the Old Testament people of God and then the addition 'who are also believers incorporate in Christ Jesus', but the use of *hagioi* in the address of other Pauline letters is against this.

move beyond the limits of the purpose and control and love of Christ, nor will they turn to the world for guidance, inspiration and strength. They find all their satisfaction and their every need met in him, and not in any other place nor from any other source. This description of the Christian's life is implied in the expression being 'baptized into Christ Jesus' (Rom. 6:3), as baptism is the outward sign of entrance into such a life. It also involves the truth that the Christian's corporate existence is in the body of Christ which is his church.

2. The common Greek greeting was *chairein* (see Acts 15:23; 23:26; Jas. 1:1); here Paul uses the cognate word *charis* (*grace*). *Peace* was the common Hebrew greeting (*shalōm*). It was used, for example, when the seventy were sent out by the Lord (Lk. 10:5). As in all his greetings, Paul brings grace and peace together, and the two may be said to sum up all the gifts of Christ. The greeting has thus become a blessing, or a prayer that his readers may know fully the free, undeserved favour of God, restoring them to himself, and adding to them all that they need (see further on 3:2 for *charis*); and that they may know peace with God, peace in their hearts, and peace with one another. The two words are in fact twin themes of the letter, as of the gospel of Christ itself. The grace and peace come *from God our Father*, as the source of all things, *and the Lord Jesus Christ*, who by what he has done has brought them to humanity.

B. PRAISE FOR GOD'S PURPOSE AND BLESSINGS IN CHRIST (1:3-14)

3. Now, after his brief greeting, and before he expresses his thanks for the welfare of those to whom he is writing (vv. 15–16), the apostle goes straight into a great paean of praise – one long sentence, impossible to analyse, in which each successive thought crowds in on the one before. There is no predetermined order in the enumeration of the blessings; the contemplation of one leads naturally to the next – election from the very beginning; sonship by adoption; redemption, which means forgiveness; insight into God's all-embracing purpose; the privilege (both for Jews and Gentiles) of becoming his people; and the sealing of the Spirit, which is the guarantee of the final inheritance. Three particular notes sound right through this great doxology. First, from eternity to eternity God works all things according to his perfect plan. All history, all people, all that exists in heaven and on earth are included in his purpose. Past, present and future are all embraced in this doxology, and the work of Father, Son and Holy Spirit. Secondly, that purpose is fulfilled in Christ, and thus in him every blessing that men and women can have is found. Thirdly, its goal is the very practical one, that God's people should live 'to the praise of his glorious grace' (v. 6).

The paragraph begins in the form of a Jewish benediction. In the New Testament the word *blessed* (*eulogētos*) is used only of God. He alone is worthy to be blessed. People are blessed when they receive his blessings; God is blessed when he is praised for all that he freely bestows on humanity and on his world. Above all he is blessed as *the God and Father of our Lord Jesus Christ* (*cf.* Rom. 15:6; 1 Pet. 1:3; Rev. 1:6); for he is revealed to us supremely in Christ who, as Son, is the perfect image of the Father (see Jn. 1:18 and Heb. 1:1–3).

The Greek translated *who has blessed* is an aorist participle, which may refer to a particular occasion in the past when those blessings were first received, or when he brought them to humanity; but the tense is not of necessity to be pressed. *With every spiritual blessing* suggests that from him comes one continuous flow of blessing, and this is to be conceived, not chiefly in terms of the material gifts of which we think most readily, but in terms of the spiritual that transcend but include the material, for the true appreciation of the things we see is dependent on our enjoyment of the things of the Spirit.

This is made clearer still by the defining phrase that follows, *in the heavenly places*. The phrase speaks of an 'invisible spiritual environment, as contrasted with the visible, tangible environment we call earth. It is the realm of all the unseen forces, good and evil, which struggle to dominate the individual and corporate life' of humanity (Caird). Five times the phrase is used in this letter. Christ is said to be exalted to be 'in the heavenly places' (1:20); the wisdom of God is being made known to the principalities and powers 'in the heavenly places' (3:10); the same phrase is used of the sphere of the spiritual conflict against the forces of evil (6:12); and, most closely connected with the subject here, in 2:6 Christians are said to be 'raised up' and made to 'sit with him in the heavenly places in Christ Jesus'. Their life is lifted above the commonplace. It is in the world, but it is also in heaven, unlimited by the material things that pass away (*cf.* Phil. 3:20). Life now, if it is life *in Christ*, is in the heavenly realm.

4. The purpose of God is shown to be not of this earth but of heaven by the fact that it existed *before the foundation of the world.* Election, as Calvin said, is 'the foundation and first cause' of all blessings. And the doctrine of election runs through the whole Bible. Israel was chosen, not for any merit, but to be the means of the fulfilling of the eternal purpose of God (see Dt. 7:6–8; Is. 42:1; 43:20–21). In the New Testament the principle of election is confirmed, but there is no longer a national limitation – a truth that this letter later develops and expounds. This doctrine of election, or predestination, is not raised as a subject of controversy or speculation. It is not set in opposition to the self-evident fact of human free will. It involves a paradox that the New Testament does not seek to resolve, and that our finite minds cannot fathom. Paul emphasizes both the sovereign purpose of God and our free will. He took the gospel of grace and offered it to all. Then to those who had accepted the gospel he set forward the doctrine of election for two reasons, both of which we find linked similarly together in John 15:16; Romans 8:29; 2 Thessalonians 2:13; 2 Timothy 1:9 and 1 Peter 1:2. Firstly, Christians need to realize that their faith rests completely on the work of God and not on the unsteady foundation of anything in themselves. It is all the Lord's work, and in accordance with his plan, a plan that reaches back *before the foundation of the world.* There is, therefore, no place for human boasting. Secondly, God has chosen us *that we should be holy and blameless before him* (*cf.* 5:27 and Col. 1:22). Election is not simply to salvation, but to holiness of life. We were 'created in Christ Jesus', 2:10 is to express it, 'for good works, which God prepared beforehand, that we should walk in them'. We were 'predestined to be conformed to the image of his Son' (Rom. 8:29).

The ideal and goal of the Christian life, therefore, is perfect holiness (*cf.* Mt. 5:48), expressed in its positive aspect as dedication of life (see on v. 1), and negatively as freedom from every fault. Behind the word *amōmous,* used similarly in Philippians 2:15, and here translated *blameless* (RV 'without blemish'), lies a use in connection with Old Testament sacrifices. Only a perfect animal could be offered to God (*e.g.* see Lv. 1:3, 10). So, as Hebrews 9:14 puts it, Christ offered himself morally and spiritually 'without blemish' to God (*cf.* 1 Pet. 1:19). The life of the Christian is also to be 'without blemish', not merely by human standards but *before him* who is the witness of all that anyone does, and thinks, and says. (For this same emphasis of the apostle on human life lived every moment in the sight of God, see Rom. 1:9; 2 Cor. 4:2; Gal. 1.20; 1 Thes. 2:5.)

5. The words *in love* may be taken either with what follows or with what precedes, and the differing opinions of translators and commentators ancient and modern indicate that it is not possible to be dogmatic regarding the intention of the writer. RSV translates *He destined us in love to be his sons* (*cf.* NIV). This may be right; at least it is a truth that this whole section emphasizes. But the position of the phrase, and its use elsewhere in the letter for human love rather than God's love (3:17; 4:2, 16; 5:2), support the rendering accepted by the AV, RV and NEB. The point, then, is that holiness of life is only made perfect in and through love (*cf.* 1 Thes. 3:12–13).

For *destined* RV has 'foreordained'; the Greek *proorisas* means literally 'marked out beforehand'. It is simply another word that expresses the fact that God's plan for his people is from eternity. That plan is, as AV literally renders it, 'the adoption of children by Jesus Christ to himself'. Men and women were created for life in fellowship with God, as children with the Father (Gn. 1:26; Acts 17:28). By sin that privilege was forfeited, but by grace, in and through Christ, restoration to sonship is made possible (Jn. 1:12). Adoption is the best way to describe this (*cf.* Rom. 8:15, 23; Gal. 4:5), because adopted children have their position by grace and not by right, and yet are brought into the family on the same footing as children by birth.

What God has done was *according to the purpose of his will.* Both expressions here speak of his purpose and sovereign love. *Purpose (eudokia)* has two meanings in Scripture. It is sometimes the goodwill felt towards a person (*cf.* Lk. 2:14); but where there is no reference to a person who feels this goodwill, it means simply 'purpose', as fits the context here and in verse 9 (*cf.* Mt. 11:26) – though there may be a suggestion of the first meaning as well. Markus Barth (*AB*) puts it, 'The happiness that accompanies a radiant good will is implied. Those singing God's praise . . . respond to God's pleasure in doing good.'

6. In this verse we have the phrase *to the praise of his glorious grace*, which occurs again in this section in verses 12 and 14 as 'the praise of his glory' – like the refrain at the end of successive stanzas of a poem. Translating the noun in Greek by the adjective *glorious* may lose some of the force. God's glory implies his revelation of himself, and 'the glory of his grace' (AV) is 'his self-disclosure as a gracious God' (Stott; *cf.* Ex. 33:18–19; 34:5–7). As Israel was chosen to live to his praise (Is. 43:21), so those who in Christ are received as his people must show forth the Father's nature of grace and thus glorify him (*cf.* 5:1; Mt. 5:45; Lk.6:35). The word *grace* is too full of meaning for Paul to pass over lightly (*cf.* v. 7 and 2:7). It must be qualified. The Greek verb *charitoō*, used in the clause *which he freely bestowed on us in the Beloved*, is from the noun *charis (grace)*. (*Cf.* the constructions in vv. 19, 20; 2:4 and 4:1.) Sometimes it has been taken to mean 'the grace with which he has made us gracious'; so Chrysostom (quoted by Abbott) says, 'it is as if one were to take a leper and change him into a lovely youth'. But it is more in accord with the context to take it as 'the favour with which he has favoured us', or, as RSV, the *grace which he freely bestowed on us*. It is the objective grace of God which is in mind, God's undeserved favour towards us, rather than any virtue that we derive.

This, it is emphasized again, is *in* Christ who is *the Beloved*. The description was used as a name for Israel, and so came to be used as a title of Israel's greatest representative, the Messiah. But its literal meaning is not lost (*cf.* Mt. 3:17 and 17:5) as the parallel expression in Colossians 1:13 – 'the Son of his love' (RV) – indicates. As Dale puts it, 'Christ dwells for ever in the infinite love of God, and as we are in Christ, the love of God for Christ is in a wonderful manner ours.'

7. The blessing of *redemption* follows, for our prior need of grace is of redeeming, restoring grace. Such redemption is found *in* Christ – not merely through him, but by coming to live *in him* (*cf.* Rom. 3:24; Col. 1:14). Again the Old Testament provides the background for our understanding. There, provision was made for the redemption of lands or persons that had passed from their original owner to become the property of another (see Lv. 25:25–27, 47–49; Nu. 18:15). The people of Israel, moreover, were themselves essentially a redeemed people. They had been slaves in Egypt, and later, through their own sinfulness, in Babylon as well. Yet God had redeemed them, and by redemption they were made his people (Ex. 15:13; Dt. 7:8; Is. 48:20; 52:9). The fundamental idea of redemption is that of the setting free of a thing or a person that has come to belong to another. Sometimes, in both Old and New Testaments, there is no specific reference to the price paid for redemption, and in some places the word has the basic sense of release (*e.g.* Lk. 21:28; Rom. 8:23; Heb. 9:15). But Paul's mind often dwelt on the thought of the costliness of redemption, and in a number of places in the New Testament this is obviously present (see Acts 20:28; 1 Cor. 6:20; 1 Pet. 1:18–19; Rev. 5:9).

We cannot say here that Paul speaks explicitly of the cost of redemption, but he says immediately that it is *through his blood.* Nor would he have hesitated to say that what is the means of liberation is in fact also the price. In the case of the Passover, a sacrifice was associated with the redemption of the people. The primary object of most of the old sacrifices, however, was the setting aside of sin. Instilled deeply into the consciousness of the people was the fact that sin could not be set aside lightly. Sin required sacrifice: 'without the shedding of blood there is no forgiveness of sins' (Heb. 9:22; *cf.* Lv. 17:11). Christ fulfilled the need expressed throughout the Old Testament sacrificial system. His death means that *blood* has been shed as a sacrifice for sin; it may also be described in terms of sin's defeat and so the release of men and women from its bondage. The sacrifice is thus the means of redemption which is *the forgiveness of our trespasses.* Sin involves the bondage of mind and will and members, but forgiveness is freedom, and *aphesis*, the word used here, means literally the loosing of a person from that which binds. This forgiveness, Paul says, is *according to the riches of his grace*, grace which is rich beyond human understanding and infinitely beyond any earthly wealth (*cf.* Mt. 6:19–20; 1 Tim. 6:17–19; Heb. 11:26). Six times in this letter the apostle speaks thus of the riches of God, revealed and made available, the wealth of his grace and mercy and glory (v. 18; 2:4, 7; 3:8, 16), and the expression is characteristically Pauline (*cf.* Rom. 2:4; 9:23; 11:33; 2 Cor. 8:9; Col. 1:27; 2:2). And God's giving is not merely out of these *riches* but *according to* their measure (*cf.* Phil. 4:19).

8. Not yet, however, are the epithets of grace exhausted. God *lavished* his grace *upon us*. The Greek verb used expresses the superabundance of God's giving, the overflow as of a fountain from a deep and abundant source; and also, by his grace, there is implied the quality expected in a Christian's life (1 Thes. 3:12; 4:1, 10).

9. The words *in all wisdom and insight* present the fourth of the great blessings which the apostle enumerates. God not only receives and forgives. Those whom he has reconciled to himself as children he also enlightens with the understanding of his purpose. RSV connects the phrase here with what follows; other translations link it with what precedes. It makes little difference to the essential meaning. In many classical writers a distinction is made between 'wisdom (*sophia*) and 'insight' (*phronēsis*). It is not always maintained, but probably it is right in this passage to distinguish *wisdom*, which Robinson defines as 'the knowledge which sees into the heart of things, which knows them as they really are', from *insight* which he calls 'the understanding which leads to right action'. If this is correct, it follows that the wisdom of God is not merely intellectual or academic, a higher philosophy such as that which the Gnostics in the early days of the church boasted that they possessed; it is also the source of understanding in the details of daily living (*cf.* Phil. 1:9–10). As Barclay puts it, 'Christ gives to men the ability to see the great ultimate truths of eternity and to solve the problems of each moment of time.'

Such *wisdom* and *insight* are possible because God reveals *his will* concerning the goal and purpose of life, and concerning its details (*cf.* Col. 1:9). What he makes known the apostle calls the *mystery*. In classical Greek the word *mystērion* had two meanings. It could mean a secret rite or secret knowledge into which one was initiated, or a secret of any kind. In the Septuagint it is used of what is revealed by God (*e.g.* Dn. 2:19), and also of the secret that a tale-bearer tells (*e.g.* Ecclus. 22:22). Apocalyptic writers speak of 'mysteries . . . prepared in heaven, but they will only be revealed at the end of history. . . . At Qumran . . . mysteries could also refer to events which were already being realized in the community.' So Lincoln comments that Paul could draw on 'the rich Semitic background of the term'.[1] Thus its Christian use is not to be regarded as derived from its use in the heathen mystery cults so common in New Testament days. Paul could not have failed, however, to think of this use, and no doubt he consciously compared with the strange and baseless heathen mysteries the truth of God in Christ revealed to all who would receive it, and given to his church to proclaim to the world. For Paul, the essential mystery was the way in which God through Christ brings men and women back into fellowship with himself. More than that, it is the way in which he brings into a restored unity the whole universe that has been disordered by human rebellion and sin. Thus the word in the New Testament conveys the thought not of something mysterious, but something revealed, and regularly words expressive of disclosure rather than keeping secret go with *mystērion* (*cf.* Col. 1:26; 2:2; 4:3). Nevertheless the word does bear the significance of truth not previously known but now revealed (Rom. 16:25), and the even more important fact that understanding depends on God's will to reveal, and on human desire to receive insight that itself must be God-given.

Then in the end of this verse we see that, just as in verses 7 and 8 the apostle sought to describe and extol in so many ways the munificence of God's grace, here he wants to express the wonder of his purpose. He does so by using three synonyms (two of them have been used already in v. 5), thus describing the *mystery* as *his will*, *his purpose*, and that which is *set forth in Christ*.

---

[1] Lincoln, p. 143.

10. In this sovereign plan what God has done and is doing in Christ is spoken of as *a plan for the fullness of time* – 'to be put into effect when the time was ripe' (NEB). Simpson aptly renders it the divine 'programme of history'. We must, however, study the word translated *plan* to see more clearly the apostle's meaning. The word here (*oikonomia*) is one that was used either for the administration of a household (*oikos*), or for the responsibility of the one who administered it. It is used several times in the New Testament in this latter sense of stewardship. For the church is the household of God, Jesus Christ is the chief steward, and under him his ministers are called to serve as stewards (see 1 Cor. 4:1–2; 9:17; Tit. 1:7; 1 Pet. 4:10). Here it is the government or arrangement of things for God's people, and for the whole universe, that is in view. Jesus Christ orders everything in its full time, and in infinite wisdom orders the time of all things. It is also to be noted here that the word used for *time* is not *chronos* which connotes the passage of time in days and months and years, but *kairos* which speaks of particular times, the decisive times of fulfilment in the purposes of God. Bruce well paraphrases: 'When all the times and seasons which the Father has fixed by His own authority have run their course, God's age-long purpose which He planned in Christ will attain its full fruition.'[1]

For the Greek word *anakephalaiōsasthai*, RSV has *unite*. The word was used of gathering things together and presenting them as a whole. The Greek practice was to add up a column of figures and put the sum at the top, and this name was given to the process. So the word was used in rhetoric for summing up an address at the end, and thus showing the relation of each part to the complete argument. In Romans 13:9 it is used for the summing up of the commandments in the one demand of love. Three ideas are present in the word here – restoration, unity, and the headship of Christ.[2] Weymouth brings out all three when he translates 'the purpose . . . of restoring the whole creation to find its one Head in Christ'. All things were created in Christ (Col. 1:16). Through sin endless disorder and disintegration have come into the world;

[1] Bruce (*EE*), p. 33.

[2] J. Barr in *The Semantics of Biblical Language* (Oxford, 1961), pp. 237f., criticizes the taking of any aspect of meaning from *kephalē* rather than just *kephalaion*, but in a letter where Christ is spoken of as head (*kephalē*) we may question whether the thought would have been absent from the writer's mind in the use of *anakephalaiōsasthai* here.

but in the end all things will be restored to their intended function and to their unity by being brought back to the obedience of Christ (cf. Col. 1:20).

The phrase *all things*, which in Greek expresses absolute universality (cf. Col. 1:17; Heb. 1:3), is qualified by *things in heaven and things on earth*. Paul has in view the whole creation, spiritual and material. At the time of writing he was concerned with a heresy in Asia Minor, which placed many spiritual powers in opposition to Christ, and others as mediators between God and humanity. His answer to such teaching – explicit in Colossians and only implicit in this letter – is that there is one alone who can and will reconcile and unify all things. It is a heresy of our times to divide life into sacred and secular. Christ is concerned in all things, and all will find their true place and unity in him. This letter, moreover, does not merely speak of a distant goal, but presents the ongoing task of the church in a world divided by barriers of race, colour, culture and political system, as that of bringing all things and all people into the captivity of obedience to Christ (cf. 2 Cor. 10:5), and so back to find their true functions and unity in him.

This verse has been used as the keystone of the doctrine of 'universalism', that all people shall be saved in the end. It does imply that in the end everything and every being in existence will be under his authority, but it is dangerous to press a doctrine from a verse without regard for the balance of the evidence of Scripture as a whole and, in this case, without respect for the solemn presentation from one end of Scripture to the other of the alternatives of life and death dependent on the acceptance or rejection of God's salvation.

11-12. The closing phrase of verse 10 in the Greek reiterates that the blessing mentioned there, like the others, is received *in* Christ. The same applies to the next phrase, for Paul continues, *In him . . . we . . . have been destined and appointed. . . .* Basically the verb here, *klēroō*, means 'choose by lot'. Often in its use the idea of the 'lot' disappeared and the thought is essentially that which recurs frequently in the Old Testament when Israel is spoken of as God's portion (see Dt. 4:20; 9:29; Zc. 2:12). The word 'inheritance' (*klēronomia*; see v. 14) is a cognate word, and it follows (through it is not exactly what is expressed here) that those who are God's portion have their inheritance in him. At this point Paul is speaking of the Old Testament beginning of the outworking of God's purpose for mankind, as he says that *we*, the Jews, became his people. 'We have been appropriated' M. Barth (*AB*) puts it.

The change of personal pronouns in this letter between first and second persons several times signifies the difference between Jews and Gentiles. Such is the case here. The divine plan for the world's redemption began with the Jews *who first hoped in Christ*. They were *destined*, 'marked out beforehand' (the word has been used in v. 5), to have a part in his purpose. And that destiny is not, as it were, blueprints of history, which are followed out automatically as the years and centuries pass by. It is the purpose of the personal God who is active in the world, working out his own will in wisdom and grace (*cf.* Rom. 8:28). Such is the force of the words used here: first, he *accomplishes* (*energountos*) or 'energizes' *all things*; then his *counsel* or determined plan (*boulē; cf.* Acts 2:23; 4:28; 13:36; 20:27); then his wish or *will* (*thelēma*; see on vv. 5 and 9). Thus NIV translates, he 'works out everything in conformity with the purpose of his will'; NEB 'as was decreed in his design whose purpose is everywhere at work'.

The goal of this his plan for the Jews, the apostle says, was that they should *live for the praise of his glory*. For no other purpose did God choose Abraham, and work out his design in the history of Israel, than that they should show forth in the world his glory (Is. 43:21), his revealed character and nature (see on v. 6). The verb translated *first hoped* has the prefix *pro-* which may mean either that they hoped in Christ before others (but after the incarnation), or that they had set their hope on Christ before he came. The fact that the Jews had the knowledge of the gospel before the Gentiles is expressed in Romans 1:16; 2:9–10. It is more likely, however, that the reference here is to the Jewish hope in 'the Christ' (Gk. has the article) before he came (*cf.* Acts. 28:20). As Scott comments, 'Ages before Christ had appeared they had known that he was coming and had been looking forward to him. Their religion, in the last resort, had turned on the hope for Christ. . . .'

13. In the Greek there is no verb in the opening relative clause of this verse. AV may be right in repeating the verb that immediately precedes. Alternatively, we may go back to the verb of verse 11, 'we have obtained an inheritance' (AV); or we can look on to the verb that comes later in this verse, as does RSV. Perhaps none of these is exactly what was intended and we may come closest to the meaning by supplying the verb 'to be'. 'And so it was with you also' (TEV). NIV has, 'And you also were included in Christ'. Gentiles without hope before (see 2:12) have come into the same purpose as the Jews, and for the same reasons. For Paul goes on to say what that involves for them.

The Gentiles had come into the purpose of God, because they had come to know Jesus as the Christ; and this transforming knowledge is described in two ways. Firstly, they had *heard the word of truth*, *i.e.* the word that brought them the knowledge of ultimate reality, the revelation of God in his Son (*cf.* 4:21; Col. 1:5). And secondly, that truth was *the gospel* or good news, because it was not only revelation, but also the message of the love and mercy and *salvation* of God for sinful humanity (*cf.* Rom. 1:16).

Hearing this word is vital, because by hearing alone comes the knowledge of the truth of the gospel (Rom. 10:14). But hearing is vain unless it leads to faith, the means by which alone God's blessings can be received. Thus Gentiles as well as Jews, having *heard* and *believed*, have been *sealed*. In the ancient world the seal was the personal sign of the owner or the sender of something important, and thus, as in a letter, it distinguished what was true from what was spurious. It was also the guarantee that the thing sealed had been carried intact. In New Testament times certain religious cults followed the practice of having their devotees tattooed with the emblem of the cult, and the initiates were then said to have been sealed. This may have been in Paul's mind here, and in the very different context of Galatians 6:17, but not necessarily so. The Jews thought of circumcision as a seal (see Rom. 4:11). The Holy Spirit is the Christian's seal. The experience of the Holy Spirit in their lives is the final proof to them, and indeed a demonstration to others, of the genuineness of what they have believed, and provides the inward assurance that they belong to God as children (*cf.* Rom. 8:15–16; Gal. 4:6). Later on, perhaps because of the analogy of circumcision, perhaps because of the language used for initiation in the mystery cults, baptism came to be known as the seal of the Spirit. It is indeed 'an outward and visible sign' given to Christians of the inward work of God, but here it is clearly intended that the Holy Spirit's presence is the seal. The Spirit in believers' lives is the undeniable mark of God's work in and for them. He is also the means by whom Christians can be kept 'intact' till the day of the Lord. (It should be noticed that the contexts here and in 4:30 and in 2 Cor. 1:21–22, where the 'seal' is spoken of, all point forward to the full possession of God's blessings in the end.) The Greek in this verse might be translated 'having believed you were sealed . . .' and be taken to suggest a two-stage experience, believing and then later being sealed by the Spirit. The participle, however, can be what is spoken of as a 'coincident aorist participle', its reference being to the same time as that of the main verb. Whatever varieties of experience there may be, the New Testament norm is that the Holy Spirit is received as one turns to the Lord in repentance and faith (as indicated in Acts 2 and in the question in Acts 19:2).

The promised Holy Spirit is the way that RSV and other translations understand the Greek which is literally the 'holy Spirit of promise' (AV). The meaning may be the Spirit as promised in the Old Testament (e.g. Ezk. 36:26–27; 37:1–14; Joel 2:28–29), and then by the Lord (Lk. 24:49; Jn. 14 – 16; Acts 1:4–5). If this is the meaning it is a little strange that Paul did not simply use the participle. It seems more likely that he meant the Holy Spirit whose presence carries the promise of good things to come, and this is the thought that is developed in the metaphors of verse 14.

14. In a bargain between two parties a 'part payment' (*arrabōn* – a word that came into Gk. from Phoenician traders) was made, which was the *guarantee* or assurance that full payment would be made. The Greek word is used three times in the Septuagint of Genesis 38:17–20 for a pledge, and significantly the same word is used in modern Greek for an engagement ring (Bruce, *EE*). Christians' experience of the Spirit now is a foretaste and pledge of what will be theirs when they fully possess their God-given inheritance. (*Cf.* 2 Cor. 1:21–22 – where it is also linked with the word 'seal' – 2 Cor. 5:5; and also Rom. 8:23 where, with a similar meaning, the Spirit is called 'the first fruits'.)

The difficult phrase that follows is translated by RSV *until we acquire possession of it*. The word in the Greek here is usually translated 'redemption' and so the thought may continue from what precedes: we have the *guarantee* now and we will have full possession later. There is, however, another meaning that is possible, since the two words 'redemption' (*apolytrōsis*) and *possession* (*peripoiēsis*), like many terms in this section, are technical terms that may be interpreted most naturally in the light of their Old Testament use which Christians were making their own. The 'redemption' is the setting free of the slaves of sin for them to become God's people. It has been so used in verse 7, and often in the New Testament it has this meaning. Such redemption is said to be partly achieved now, but in the end will be achieved fully (see 4:30; Rom. 8:23; Lk. 21:28); God will then take completely from alien hands that which is his own. The object redeemed could thus be understood as 'those who are God's possession' (NIV), and this expression is used in 1 Peter 2:9 calling to mind Exodus 19:5 and perhaps Isaiah 43:21 and Malachi 3:17.[1] Thus RV translates 'unto the redemption of God's own possession'; and NEB 'when God has redeemed what is his own'. If we follow this, we must assume that 'the metaphor from a mercantile transaction has by this time been wholly dropped' (Robinson) and the Old Testament metaphors, more readily in the mind of an apostle, taken up again. In either case this great doxology ends with the thought of the full possession of all that God has planned for humanity – Jews and Gentiles alike – and this, like all that has been given at each stage in the unfolding of God's purpose, is *to the praise of his glory.*

C. PRAYER FOR DIVINE ENLIGHTENMENT (1:15–23)

15. After the great doxology of verses 3–14, the apostle's mind turns to those to whom he is writing. He now gives thanks and prays for them, but this also is not simply in the conventional manner of contemporary letter-writing (see on v. 1) but in the spirit of true Christian prayer. In particular – as the opening *For this reason* signifies – he prays in the light of the wealth of spiritual blessing of which he has just been writing. The thought of the purpose of God in Christ, the blessings of election, sonship,

[1] See Robinson, p. 148.

redemption, revelation, the gift of the Holy Spirit, leads naturally and inevitably to praise and prayer for the members of his church (*cf.* 3:14).

Paul had *heard* of the fruit of the gospel among his readers, perhaps in the same way as he had heard of it in the church at Colossae (Col. 1:6–8). As we have seen,[1] the lack of more specific and detailed thanksgivings here, even such as Paul wrote to churches that he had never visited (Rom. 1:8; Col. 1:3–9), argues strongly against Ephesus, or Ephesus alone, being the original destination planned for this letter. At the same time the writer has definite readers in view, and can give thanks for their *faith in the Lord Jesus*, the basic thing that can lead to the experience of all that the same Lord Jesus seeks to do and to give. Nor is this *faith* a matter only of their personal relation to their Lord. It affects their conduct towards *all the saints*. RSV, NIV and NEB have here the word *love* which is omitted by the RV following some ancient MSS. The UBS and Nestlé Greek Testaments include the word for *love*, but it is a little more likely that love was added to the original text (in agreement with Col. 1:4 and Phm. 5) than omitted by a copyist's slip, though its absence gives an expression without parallel in the New Testament. There is also a difficulty in using the same word *faith* in a different sense with the two objects that follow. The apostle may have spoken of their outgoing, undiscriminating love toward all the saints, and the words have dropped out from some MSS in error. Otherwise his meaning must be that their faith was evident, not only in their inward spiritual lives but in their relationships with all their fellow-Christians as well.

16. Two features of the apostle's prayer life are in evidence in this verse. We see in the first place its constancy. Paul exhorted others to 'pray constantly' (1 Thes. 5:17; *cf.* Eph. 6:18; Rom. 12:12; Col. 4:2) and from all his letters we can form a clear impression of his earnest, unwearying prayer for 'all the churches' (see 2 Cor. 11:28 and compare the introductions of almost all his letters). Secondly, we see the place of thanksgiving in his prayer. He taught others that praise should be the unfailing accompaniment of intercession (Eph. 5:19–20; Phil. 4:6; Col. 3:15–17; 1 Thes. 5:18),

[1]See pp. 22–24.

and this also we see from his letters was a feature of his own praying. *Remembering* may be a fair translation of the Greek here, but the more specific 'making mention' (AV and RV) may be more precise.

17. He who hears and answers prayer is described firstly as *the God of our Lord Jesus Christ*. More frequently we have the title 'the God and Father of our Lord Jesus Christ' (see on v. 3), but here (where the following phrase doubtless has influenced the form of this) simply his *God*, that is, the God whom he acknowledges and whom he reveals to us. There is nothing in the expression which is contrary to his own sharing of the Godhead; for he could speak of the Father as 'my God' (Mt. 27:46; Jn. 20:17). Secondly, he is *the Father of glory*. (*Cf*. the titles 'God of glory' in Acts 7:2 and 'Lord of Glory' in 1 Cor. 2:8.) He is the Father to whom all glory belongs; for all the power and majesty revealed in creation, providence and redemption (see on v. 6) are his, and he the source. Such a thought of who God is gives to prayer a sense of awe and strengthens faith in those who pray (*cf*. 3:14ff.).

The gift, above all others, which he asks from God for his readers is *a spirit of wisdom and of revelation* (*cf*. Col. 1:9). Sometimes in the letters the word *spirit* refers to the human spirit (*e.g.* in 4:23; Rom. 1:9; 2 Cor. 7:13), or it may refer to a quality of mind or soul that a person may receive or show, in particular a spiritual attitude or endowment. So 1 Corinthians 4:21 and Galatians 6:1 speak of 'a spirit of gentleness' and 2 Corinthians 4:13 of a 'spirit of faith'. Then often, of course, it refers to the Holy Spirit of God. Robinson says, 'With the article, very generally, the word indicates the personal Holy Spirit; while without it, some special manifestation or bestowal of the Holy Spirit is signified.' So probably here we should take it as NEB 'the spiritual powers of wisdom and vision', but understand these as possible only as the gift of the Spirit who makes wise (see on v. 8), and who alone reveals the truth (Jn. 14:26; 16:13; 1 Cor. 2:12). Such wisdom and revelation, moreover, come, not simply as such higher intelligence is given from God, but by *the knowledge of him*, the personal knowledge of God himself, which in the Bible always connotes the experience of life in union and fellowship with him (see on 4:13). Paul put the prayer for wisdom first because to him the gospel was so wonderful that it was impossible for people to see the glory of it unless they were taught by God, and also because he knew that the knowledge of God was life itself (cf. Jn. 17:3; Phil. 3:10).

18. Such knowledge of God is described further, as often in both Old and New Testaments, as the enlightenment of men and women. The Old Testament gave hope for the future in terms of the coming of light into a world in darkness and as the opening of the eyes of the blind (e.g. Is. 9:2; 35:5; 42:6; 49:6; 60:1–2, 19). When Christ came his presence was described as the dawning of a new day, the breaking in of the light of God (Mt. 4:16; Lk. 1:79; Jn. 1:9; 8:12; 2 Cor. 4:6). Apart from him, or in rejection of him, the eyes of people's hearts are closed, and they are in the darkness of sin and ignorance and despair (5:8; cf. Mt. 13:15; Rom. 1:21); but those who receive him into their lives find their *eyes . . . enlightened* and made able to see (cf. Mt. 13:16–17; Acts 26:18; Heb. 6:4; 10:32). The verse speaks specifically of *the eyes of your hearts* and we need to remember that in biblical expression the heart is not simply the seat of the emotions, nor the seat of the intellect or 'understanding' (AV), but as Masson puts it 'the centre of the personality', to which God speaks, 'the inner man in his entirety' (Barry). This is clear from the study of the use of the word in the Bible, but it is evident even here when we consider what the apostle now speaks of as the results of objects of this enlightenment of the heart.

The apostle prays that by the eyes of their heart being enlightened they *may know* three things. The first is *what is the hope to which he has called you.* The apostle can speak of 'your call' (4:4), but in the desire to emphasize again that what they have depends on God's initiative, he speaks of it as 'his calling' (AV). This calling can be spoken of as having taken place in the past – God has called men and women to himself (2 Tim. 1:9); or as continuing in the present (1 Thes. 2:12; 5:24) and so involving a life-long vocation of service and sanctification (4:1; Phil. 3:14; Heb. 3:1). But also, because it is the call of the eternal God, it brings to those without hope (2:12) the expectation of an eternal destiny. This hope, moreover, is not just 'a vague and wistful longing for the triumph of goodness',[1] but it is something assured because of the present possession of the Spirit as 'the guarantee' (v. 14) and because of faithfulness of the God who has promised the future inheritance. The call of God, in other words, is effective not only in life now (*cf.* 1 Cor. 15:19) but it gives the sure promise of life with him as his people for ever, and this hope in its turn should vitally affect life for the Christian in the here and now (1 Jn. 3:2–3).

Secondly, he prays that they may know *what are the riches of his glorious inheritance in the saints*. Some have taken this to mean what God possesses in his saints. They are 'the Lord's portion' as verses 11 and 12 have shown. But the thought hardly fits the context here, nor is it in agreement with the more frequent use of the word *inheritance* in the New Testament (see v. 14; 5:5 and Col. 1:12). The preposition (*en*) here has the force of 'among' as is clear from the two close parallels to the expression of this verse in Acts 20:32 and 26:18. The fellowship of Christians is the sphere in which the inheritance of God is found, just as it is true also that it is in and through his church that the truth of God's purpose becomes known and declared (3:9–11 and 18). As people are enlightened by the Spirit of God, who is himself 'the guarantee' of the inheritance (1:14), so increasingly they realize *the riches* of that inheritance (see on v. 7), and its glory, that is, its essential quality as life in God for ever. It is to be noted also that just as it was 'his calling' (AV; not 'yours') of which the apostle spoke, so here it is *his . . . inheritance*, the inheritance from God the Father which Christians share with his Son Jesus Christ (Rom. 8:17).

19. Thirdly, the apostle prays for the enlightenment that, in addition to vision and aspiration, they may know *what is the immeasurable greatness of his power*. Once again he expresses this in the strongest terms that language can find, both by speaking of its surpassing magnitude, and by using all the synonyms possible. The four words are distinguished more clearly as they are translated in RV as 'power', 'working', strength' and 'might'. One is lost in RSV by the substitution of the adjective *great*. The

---

[1] W. M. F. Scott, *The Hidden Mystery* (London, 1942), pp. 23f.

power (dynamis) of God he would stress in particular is not just an abstract quality, but it is known *according to its working* which can be seen and realized. The Greek word here is *energeia* from which our word 'energy' comes, and the phrase used here is found again in 3:7, 4:16, Philippians 3:21 and Colossians 1:29. Moreover it is his great 'strength' *(kratos)*, that distinctive attribute of the divine nature that is praised in the New Testament doxologies (1 Tim. 6:16; 1 Pet. 4:11; 5:11; Jude 25; Rev. 1:6; 5:13); and it is his *might (ischys)* which he possesses and is also able to make available to us *(cf.* 6:10; 1 Pet. 4:11). The burden of the prayer in fact is that the mighty power of God may be known in experience by its operation *in us who believe (cf.* 3:20); and the apostle is confident that it belongs to men and women on this simple condition of their believing, that is, their laying hold of it, accepting it from him, as a gift that he wants them to have.

20. The power which thus is made available to men and women is the power demonstrated, and known in its true measure, by God's own working, power *which he accomplished in Christ*, and that in two decisive acts. Firstly, he showed this power *when he raised him from the dead.* Most frequently the New Testament describes the resurrection as the work of God the Father (see Acts 2:24, 32, etc.). His raising his Son from the dead is the mark of his approval, the acknowledgement of him as his Son, and the declaration of him as Lord of all (Acts 3:15; 4:10; 10:40; 17:31; Rom. 1:4). But it is also the manifestation of the Father's power. Secondly, that power is shown in that he 'set him at his own right hand' (AV). The ascension may not often be described in the New Testament (Mk. 16:19; Lk. 24:51; Acts 1:9), but it is constantly assumed, and its significance stressed (*e.g.* Rom. 8:34; Col. 3:1; Heb. 1:3; 1 Pet. 3:22). To Paul, and in the New Testament generally, the cross, the resurrection and the ascension are considered as three parts of one great act of God. The ascension, like the resurrection, is emphasized as being the Father's work. It is his honouring his Son with the highest possible honour (Phil. 2:9–11), but, again, it is also the demonstration of his power.

In the words here we have an allusion to Psalm 110:1, a verse often referred to in the New Testament. The exalting of the king

71

of Israel as God's anointed lent itself to a supreme application to the Christ. It was so applied before his coming, but most especially after his death and resurrection and ascension (Acts 2:34-35; Heb. 1:13; and see also Mt. 26:64; Acts 7:55; Rom. 8:34; Col. 3:1; Heb. 1:3; 8:1; 10:12; 12:2; 1 Pet. 3:22). Inevitably as the ascension and exaltation of Christ are referred to we have spatial imagery, but as Calvin puts it, when it is said that he is lifted up to the Father's right hand, 'It does not mean any particular place, but the power which the Father hath bestowed on Christ, that he may administer in his name the government of heaven and earth'.

Thus the resurrection and ascension, as well as indicating that the work of Christ on earth was finished, express the measure of the Father's power made available to humanity. The apostle prayed for himself 'that I may know him and the power of his resurrection' (Phil. 3:10). Often he thought of these mighty acts of God not only as the measure of the power that Christians can possess but as indicating the divine strength that can raise them to new life with Christ (1 Cor. 6:14; 2 Cor. 4:14; Col. 2:12), and make them live *in the heavenly places* (see on v. 3) with him. But this latter thought is developed more fully in the next section (2:6).

21. Now the thought of the resurrection and exaltation of Christ leads rather to the declaration of him as Lord of all. His position is *far above all rule and authority and power and dominion.* Such was always his place in the universe because he is eternally God the Son (Jn. 3:31). To it he was exalted again after he had humbled himself to assume our humanity (Eph. 4:10). The titles in this verse may have been taken as those of the spiritual powers venerated by such teachers as those who were opposed by the apostle in Colossians. Three of the four used here are found in the plural in Colossians 1:16, where it is asserted that Christ is the creator of every spiritual power there is. Here Paul is concerned to affirm that Christ is Lord over them all; he is *above every name that is named*, every dignity that is reverenced by human beings (*cf.* Phil. 2:9). There are powers *not only in this age but also in that which is to come*: the apostle would thus far agree with the Gnostics. But he would assert that none of these has any being apart from Christ; all of them that are evil have been vanquished by him (Col. 2:15), and all are subject to him as Lord (*cf.* Rom. 8:38; 1 Pet. 3:22). Against the spiritual powers of evil the servants of Christ must do battle in their Master's strength (Eph. 6:12), and also Paul will say that to 'the principalities and powers in the heavenly places' the church is uniquely to declare 'the manifold wisdom of God' (3:10).

The contrast between *this age* and the age to come was common in the Rabbis and often implied in the New Testament (*e.g.* in Lk. 16:8; 20:34; Rom. 12:2; 1 Cor. 2:6; Heb. 6:5). Together they may, as here and in Matthew 12:32, make an all-embracing whole.

22. What has gone before may be summed up by saying that the Father *has put all things under his feet*, and so, doubtless intentionally, the words of Psalm 8:6 are used. This verse is used again in 1 Corinthians 15:27, and it is important to notice that the Psalm speaks of the place of humanity as God intended it to be, crowned 'with glory and honour' and given 'dominion over the works' of God's hands (Ps. 8:5–6). In a great measure this position was lost and men and women brought into bondage by sin. Therefore we see one only, the true man Jesus Christ, fulfilling this divine purpose; but through him and in him we are restored to our true dignity. Hebrews 2:5–10 may be regarded as an inspired commentary on Psalm 8 as fulfilled in Christ, and in those who through him are brought as 'sons to glory'.[1]

Jesus Christ is Lord over all, but in particular this is his relationship to the church, for the Father *made him the head over all things for the church*. In recent studies[2] of the word *kephale* (*head*) it has been stressed that it often has the sense of 'origin' and thus it could be taken here as meaning that 'Christ is divinely appointed as source of the church's life' (Bruce, *NICNT*). The context, however, is surely against this, as verse 21

[1] It is significant that in both 1 Corinthians 15 and Hebrews 1 – 2, as in this passage, Psalm 8 and Psalm 110 are linked together.

[2] See S. Bedale, 'The meaning of kephalē in the Pauline Epistles' in *JTS* (new series) 5 (1954), pp. 211–215, and compare H. Schlier in *TDNT*, 3, pp. 679–681 and G. Howard, 'The Head/Body Metaphors of Ephesians' in *NTS* 20 (1973–74), pp. 350–356.

and the earlier part of this verse have clearly stressed the Lordship of Christ.

We should note, however, that the apostle does not simply speak of him as given to be head of the church – Lord of all, and of the church in particular – but that he is 'supreme head' (NEB) or more literally head over all things 'to' or 'for' the church. There is given to the church, and for the church's benefit, a head who is also head over all things. The church has authority and power to overcome all opposition because her leader and head is Lord of all. Jesus himself had authority because he was under the Father's authority; he was doing his will and therefore had all the authority of God (see Mt. 8:9–10; 11:27; Jn. 17:2). Such authority he passes on to his disciples, in as much as they go out in his name, in obedience to him, and to do his work (Mt. 28:18–20; Mk. 3:14–15; Jn. 20:21–23).

23. For the church's benefit Christ is the head, and his great purpose for the church and its relationship to him is expressed by speaking of it as *his body*. This is a most revealing term for the church, peculiarly Pauline (2:16; 4:4, 12, 16; 5:30; Rom. 12:5; 1 Cor. 10:17; 12:27; Col. 1:24; 2:19), though the essential truth behind its use is found in other New Testament writers. It means more than saying that the church is the company of the disciples of Christ, the people of God; it expresses the essential union of his people with him (as in the parable of the vine and the branches in John 15) – the same life of God flows through all; and it speaks of the whole as functioning in obedience to him, carrying out his work in the world.

This designation of the function of the church is amplified yet further; it is not only his body, it is intended to be *the fullness of him who fills all in all*. We may paraphrase this by saying that it is God's purpose that the church should be the full expression of Jesus Christ, who himself fills everything there is. Colossians 1:19 and 2:9 speak of all the divine fullness indwelling Christ himself, that is to say he is filled by, and is the full expression of, the Godhead.[1] Colossians 2:10 continues 'you have come to

---

[1] Caird takes the 'fullness' in this passage to speak of Christ, not the church, but that is grammatically difficult. See further the special note on *plērōma* in C. F. D. Moule, *CGT*, on Colossians and Philemon, pp. 164ff.

fullness of life in him'. In this sense Christians are intended to be 'filled with all the fullness of God' (3:19; and *cf.* Jn. 1:14, 16), that is, to receive the fullness of the attributes and gifts of God that it is possible for people to receive. In this same way 4:13 describes the Christian's growth to spiritual maturity as development 'to the measure of the stature of the fullness of Christ'.

Another interpretation of these words, understood by many ancient versions in their translation of the Greek, and followed by many commentators, is that in some sense the church fills Christ, and he is made complete by the church. Robinson paraphrases, 'so the Christ may have no part lacking, but may be wholly completed and fulfilled'. So Calvin says, 'Until he is united to us, the Son of God reckons himself in some sense imperfect.' There are several reasons for this being taken as the meaning. It is felt that it gives a truer meaning of the word *fullness* (*plērōma*), that which fills, rather than that which is filled. Also the form of the participle translated *who fills* by RSV is the Greek middle or passive voice, and not active as is the verb in 4:10. On the other hand the meaning of *plērōma* (by formation a *passive* noun) seems to be best taken from the passages quoted above, and in particular the phrase in 4:13 strongly favours the sense in which we have taken it here. If the participle were passive we could not translate it as RSV and many other translations do; but if middle, the meaning would be much the same as the active.[1] As H. C. G. Moule (*CB*) puts it, the middle 'suggests intensity and richness of action; a power which is indeed living and life-giving'. Nowhere in the New Testament is it said that Christ finds his fullness and fulfilment in the church. (The nearest that we come to such a concept is in Col. 1:24.) The reverse is the more natural idea, Christ filling all things and bringing all things to completeness of being; this fits the context here better, and it is one of the great themes of this letter (1:10; 4:10, 13, 16). As Barth (*AB*) puts it, 'the head fills the body with powers of movement and perception, and thereby inspires the

---

[1] It must be said that there is greater difficulty in the phrase *all in all* if the participle is taken as passive. In that case it must be an adverbial accusative, but this is perhaps less likely when the phrase is so closely connected with the participle by being put between it and its article.

whole body with life and direction'. The sequence of thought here seems to be: by his resurrection and ascension Christ is exalted to be Lord of all, he is head of all things for the church; the church is his body intended to express him in the world; more than that, the church is intended to be a full expression of him by being filled by him whose purpose it is to fill everything there is.[1]

II. LIFE IN CHRIST (2:1 – 3:21)

A. NEW LIFE FROM THE DEAD (2:1–10)

1. The apostle's intercession has led him to speak of the power of God shown supremely in raising his Son Jesus Christ from the dead, and to pray that his readers may know spiritual power in their lives in such measure (1:19–20). He has also spoken of their calling into his body, the church. He wants to demonstrate the great truth that Jew and Gentile are brought together into that body. But before he does so he shows that both Jew and Gentile alike have now received new life in and with the risen Christ. This section is one long sentence which, in the original, does not have its main verb till verse 5. *He made alive* is put here to make the sentence read more easily in English. In the original it begins with the object, *and you*, and as in the great exposition of salvation by Christ in Romans 1 – 8, the apostle does not show the grace of God until he has made inescapably clear the desperate need and universal sinfulness of humanity (*cf.* Col. 1:21–22).

The trouble with men and women is not merely that they are out of harmony with their environment and with their fellows. They are 'alienated from the life of God' (4:18), that is, with respect to their true spiritual nature they are *dead through . . . trespasses and sins*. There is probably no essential difference between the two nouns: the root meaning of the first is 'missing the mark' and of the second 'slipping' or 'falling from the way', and thus both express the failure of people to live as they could

---

[1] See the full discussion in Barth (*AB*), vol. 1, pp. 158f., 183ff.

and should. They were made in God's image to live as children in his family, aware of his presence, rejoicing in his direction. Freedom was given, but with it a warning that it involved the possibility of disobedience, and that disobedience would lead to death (Gn. 2:17). This death is not primarily physical death, but the loss of the spiritual life given, life in fellowship with God and the consequent capacity for spiritual activity and development. Thus the description here is not merely metaphorical, nor does it refer only to the future state of the sinners. It describes their present condition, and indeed the Bible often speaks therefore of humanity in a state of spiritual death because of sin (*e.g.* Ezk. 37:1–14; Rom. 6:23; 7:10, 24; Col. 2:13), and needing nothing less than new life from God (*cf.* Eph. 5:14; Jn. 3:3; 5:24).

2. The sinful condition of humanity is lifeless and motionless as far as any Godward activity is concerned. Viewed from another standpoint it is a 'walk', a taking of step after step, in evil (*cf.* 4:17). The Jews called their laws of conduct *Halachah*, which means 'Walking' (*cf.* Mk. 7:5; Acts 21:21; Heb. 13:9, RV mg.). This figure is used later in this letter (2:10; 4:1; 5:2, 8, 15), as elsewhere in the New Testament (*e.g.* 2 Cor. 5:7; Col. 4:5; 1 Jn. 1:6; 2 Jn. 4) for the progress of the Christian life; but here it describes a life lived according to an authority contrary to God.

This authority is expressed in three ways, in terms of its power in the world, its spiritual nature, and its activity in human lives. Firstly, it is that which is in accordance with *the course of this world*. Both of these two words, *aiōn*, translated *course* or more often 'age', and *kosmos* translated *world*, are often used in the New Testament to contrast the life of humanity apart from God, limited by earthbound motives, with that life which is lived in acknowledgment of God's kingship and with the realization of his presence (see on 1:21). Doubtless the two words are used together for emphasis here. As John Stott puts it, both words 'express a whole social value-system which is alien to God. It permeates, indeed dominates, non-Christian society and holds people in captivity. Wherever human beings are being dehumanised – by political oppression or bureaucratic tyranny, by an outlook that is secular (repudiating God), amoral (repudiating absolutes), or materialistic (glorifying the consumer market), by poverty, hunger, or unemployment, by racial discrimination or by any form of injustice – there we can detect the sub-human values of "this age" and "this world".'[1]

Then secondly, it is *following the prince of the power of the air*. By this phrase, grammatically difficult in the original, but essentially clear in meaning, the devil is described; and by speaking of the devil's authority as 'in the air', Paul was not necessarily accepting the current notion of the air being the abode and realm of evil spirits. Basically his thought was of an evil power with control in the world (see on 6:12), but whose existence was not material but spiritual.

In the third place, Paul speaks of the authority of *the spirit that is now at work in the sons of disobedience*. In this phrase there is another grammatical difficulty, but whether *spirit* depends as a genitive on *prince* or *power*, the essential meaning is clear. The old life, without the energizing of God (see 1:11 and 20) is subject to the energizing (Gk. *energountos*) of the powers of evil, controlled by *the spirit* which has the evil one as its source. For a person's inner life must be surrendered to the working of God or to that of the powers of evil (*cf.* Lk. 22:3; Jn. 13:2, 27; Acts 5:4; and especially see Lk. 11:24–26). And if people are surrendered to the power of evil, they become those whose habit of life is contrary to the living God, and so they are rightly called *the sons of disobedience* (*cf.* 5:8).

3. The apostle has begun to speak of Gentiles, but now he changes to the first person (see on 1:11) and so includes himself and *all* his people as *among* the children of disobedience (*cf.* Rom. 2:1–9; 3:9, 23). As Caird puts it, 'Paul the Pharisee would have hotly denied that the Jew was in these respects on a level with the Gentile . . . , but Paul the Christian had come to see that the possession of the law of Moses was no protection against *desires of body and mind, i.e.* the promptings of instincts and false ideas.' An alternative way of taking the relative at the beginning of the verse is with reference to trespasses and sins 'in which',

[1] Stott, p. 73.

he may have intended to say, *we all once lived*. Essentially it makes little difference to the meaning. The old way of life was a life in sin and disobedience following *the passions of our flesh*. The word 'flesh' as used in the New Testament, signifies in the first place simply the matter of the body, not inherently evil – the Word of God could become flesh (Jn. 1:14). Then it could be used to speak of the whole lower nature of man, apart from the regenerating and sanctifying Spirit of God. The biblical phrase 'the lusts of the flesh', as it is often translated, is not to be taken in too narrow a sense, but as the longings and impulses of the self-centred life (*cf*. Rom. 8:4–9; Gal. 5:16–21). Apart from their restoration to God and the indwelling of God's Spirit, men and women are not only dominated by self-centred passions, but found actually *following the desires of body and mind*. The last word translates the plural of a word more commonly used in the singular (*dianoia*) meaning a 'thought' or 'purpose', or 'intelligence'. It signifies clearly that the effects in human life of evil and selfishness are not limited to the emotions but embrace intellect and reasoning processes as well (*cf*. Col. 1:21).

Paul says finally that Jews, *like the rest of mankind* (*hoi loipoi*, as many of his own people disparagingly called the Gentiles) *were by nature children of wrath*. Many have taken this to mean that we were born with a nature that made us, even before we actually sinned, subject to the wrath of God. We would have therefore in the verse not only a doctrine of 'original sin' but of 'original guilt' or 'transmitted guilt'. It seems clear, however, that neither of the phrases *children of wrath* or *by nature* refers necessarily to the human condition from birth. *Children* here characterizes people of a certain type without special reference of necessity to their parentage or to what they have inherited from their parents. In this letter alone we have 'sons of disobedience' (2:2) and 'children of light' (5:8), and the New Testament provides other similar examples. *By nature* often refers to what is innate, to what a person is by heredity (Rom. 2:27; 11:24; Gal. 2:15), but this is not always the case. Romans 2:14, for example, shows that it can mean what people are by the habitual practices of their lives, what they are if left to themselves, not necessarily because of the inborn nature. So NEB takes it here, 'In our natural condition we, like the rest, lay under the dreadful judgement of

79

God.' Furthermore, it is asked whether what is logically prior – if 'transmitted guilt' was intended – would be set thus at the end. Instead the regular biblical order is seen – human sin, in thought and in action, and in consequence the wrath of God. In fact, we have here in just a few clauses a summing up of Paul's great treatment of sin and its consequences in Romans 1 – 3. Jew and Gentile alike have sinned against the light and the law that they have possessed and known, and so 'all the world' is 'brought under the judgement of God' (Rom. 3:19, RV).

4. Such was the plight of all mankind. *But God* broke in. We have what John Stott speaks of as 'a mighty adversative'. Set against 'the desperate condition of fallen mankind' we have 'the gracious initiative and sovereign action of God'. The subject of the verb has waited from the beginning of the chapter to this point. The verb waits till the next verse, till Paul in his usual manner (*cf.* 1:17; 3:9, 15–16), having mentioned the name of God, speaks in glowing terms of his goodness and grace. He is not only merciful, showing his pity to those who are totally unworthy and undeserving; he is *rich in mercy* (see on 1:7). That mercy proceeds from love, *the great love with which he loved us.* There is longing in the heart of God for humanity – the *us* now means Jews and Gentiles alike – to be restored to the highest and best that he had planned for them (*cf.* Jn. 3:16; 1 Jn. 4:9–10); and so he has shown himself full of mercy, and has acted in grace towards them.

5. But before the apostle describes the action of the love of God, he resumes the object and emphasizes once again our human condition and desperate need. His love reached down to us *even when we were dead through our trespasses* (*cf.* Rom. 5:6, 8), and he *made us alive together with Christ.* We have seen that new life, and nothing less, was needed. By his death and resurrection he did no less than bring 'life and immortality to light' (2 Tim. 1:10). For in his death he suffered for sin, and removed the barrier to fellowship with God that sin caused, and by his resurrection he showed his triumph over death, physical and spiritual. The forgiveness of sins means the establishment of a right relationship with God and that means new life (*cf.* Col.

2:13). Because Christ was raised from the dead, men and women are raised from being dead in sins, and have new life *with Christ* and in Christ (*cf.* Rom. 6:4–8; 8:11; 2 Cor. 4:14). The word *together*, here and twice in the next verse, is given in the Greek by adding the prepositional prefix *syn-* to the verb. Often Paul used it thus to express a union with Christ (*cf.* Rom. 6:6, 8; Col. 2:12; 2 Tim. 2:11–12), and in this case it led him apparently to coin a new word to express the new revelation. The preposition here may also carry the hint of the fact that from whatever racial or national background people have come, they are brought into this new life in Christ in fellowship together, a theme that is developed fully in the next section.[1]

This new life, as the exposition of it has shown, can also be described as salvation from sin, and Paul cannot help but add here (though he waits till later to develop it) his favourite summing up of the gospel, *by grace you have been saved*. For the human situation could be described not only in terms of spiritual death, but also as enslavement and inescapable entanglement in the coils of sin. From that bondage Christ brought liberation (*cf.* Rom. 6:12–23). The precise form of words here stresses two things. As consistently emphasized by Paul, salvation is entirely of his *grace*, his free, undeserved favour to mankind. Then also this salvation is presented as an accomplished fact. There are ways in which the New Testament can speak of salvation as a present (1 Cor. 1:18; 15:2; 2 Cor. 2:15) or a future experience (Rom. 5:9–10), since it means deliverance from the power of sin now, and in the end it will mean deliverance from the very presence of sin. But as deliverance from the penalty of sin, as free forgiveness, salvation is described by the use of the perfect tense, expressing as it does a completed action 'continuous and permanent' in its results (Robinson).

6. The recital of the work of God's grace in Christ continues in lyrical terms. Some have suspected a liturgical origin for much in these verses; at least praise and prayer in this letter are often

---

[1]It would be necesssary to take this as the force of the compound verb if the variant reading with 'in' before 'Christ' were accepted. In the next verse the phrase 'in Christ Jesus' certainly follows verbs compounded with *syn-* but probably the true reading in this verse omits 'in'.

in terms appropriate to liturgy. In 1:20 we read of the declaration of the Father's power, not only in raising Christ from the dead, but also in the fact that he 'made him sit at his right hand in the heavenly places'. So, as this chapter speaks of his quickening us together with Christ, it goes on to say that he *raised us up with him, and made us sit with him in the heavenly places in Christ Jesus.* In 1:3 the apostle has said that God has 'blessed us in Christ with every spiritual blessing in the heavenly places'. Now he says more specifically that our life has come to be there, enthroned with Christ. If this is not explicitly stated elsewhere in the Pauline letters, the meaning is implicit in such a passage as Colossians 3:1–3. Humanity, by virtue of Christ's conquest of sin and death and by his exaltation, is lifted 'from the deepest hell to heaven itself' (Calvin). Citizenship is now in heaven (Phil. 3:20); and there, and not under the limits imposed by the world, nor in conformity to its standards (Rom. 12:2), true life is found.

7. The purpose of God for his church, as Paul came to understand it, reaches beyond itself, beyond the salvation, the enlightenment and the re-creation of individuals, beyond its unity and fellowship, beyond even its witness to the world. The church is to be the exhibition to the whole creation of the wisdom and love and grace of God in Christ. (The verb used, *endeiknymi*, means 'display' [NEB] or *show* rather than simply 'make known', as its use in such passages as Rom. 2:15 and Tit. 3:2 indicates.) This has been expressed in part in 1:6, 12 and 14 where the spiritual blessings that are offered in Christ were spoken of as given and received 'to the praise of his glorious grace'. It will be expressed more specifically in 3:9–10. Here the purpose of our being raised to new life in Christ, and lifted with him to a heavenly citizenship, is said to be *that in the coming ages he might show the immeasurable riches of his grace in kindness toward us in Christ Jesus.*

Sometimes *the coming ages* have been understood to refer to successive stages or periods of this present world order. The language, though this phrase is not paralleled precisely in the New Testament, is against this. (See on 1:21 and *cf.* Mt. 12:32; Mk. 10:30.) Paul never saw this world order as such an extending vista with successive ages. It is true that in his later letters he placed less stress on the immediacy of Christ's coming again, perhaps as he saw the vastness of the unfinished task, but he never exchanged the sense of urgency for a concept of unrolling ages between himself and the Lord's coming, nor did he vary his emphasis on the need for readiness to meet the Lord at any time (see Phil. 1:10; 2:16; 3:20; 4:5 and Col. 3:4). We must allow 3:10 to help interpret this verse. The apostle's vision of the function of the church in the purpose of God has been lifted beyond this present order: as 'in the limitless future, as age succeeds age, the crowning display of God's grace will ever be His kindness to His redeemed people . . .' (Bruce, *EE*).

We should notice further that here again the word *grace* demanded qualification in terms that could show the wonder of the God who is its author (*cf.* v. 4). Once more there are shown to be *riches* of grace, the true eternal wealth (see on 1:7), *immeasurable*, exceeding, abounding, overflowing riches (the participle has been used of the power of God in 1:19) displayed towards mankind in Christ. That grace, moreover, is expressed *in kindness* (*chrēstotēs*), a word that denotes love in action (*cf.* Rom. 2:4; 11:22; Tit. 3:4), personal pity and help rendered where it was needed most.

8. Now the statement made parenthetically in verse 5 is repeated, expanded and expounded. Why can the life of heaven be possessed here and now? How is there such an exhibition of the love of God from which the whole creation of God can learn and wonder? Because *by grace you have been saved*. This salvation is God's work entirely, the bestowal of his infinite love. The human part in receiving it can be described simply by the words *through faith* (*cf.* Rom. 3:22, 25; Gal. 2:16; 1 Pet. 1:5). And this faith is defined best as a turning to God with a sense of need and weakness and emptiness and a willingness to receive what he offers, to receive the Lord himself (Jn. 1:12).

Anxious to emphasize with crystal clarity the nature of this faith and the nature of grace, Paul, by his qualifying phrases in this verse and the next, excludes the possibility of anyone obtaining this salvation by any merit or self-effort. Firstly he adds to his statement of salvation by grace through faith the words *and this is not your own doing, it is the gift of God*. Sometimes this has been taken to refer to faith itself being only possible by God's gift. If we take it this way, we would need to regard the second part of verse 8 as a parenthesis, since verse 9 must refer to the salvation and not to faith. It seems better, however, especially in the light of the parallelism between verse 8 and verse 9 (*not your own doing* . . . 'not because of works') to take all the qualifying clauses as simply emphasizing salvation by grace. What the apostle wants to say is that the whole initiative and every aspect of the making available of this salvation is God's. 'God's is the gift' is the rendering that shows best the emphasis of the word order in the Greek. 'Let a man be abandoned by God, and he is absolutely hopeless. It is the voice of God that arouses, that awakens, that causes a man to think and enquire; it is the power of God that gives strength to act; it is the same power which makes provision for the need of the new life.'[1]

9. Then, secondly, we are taken back to the terminology of Romans and Galatians – *not because of works* – and to what was a vital question for the Jews of Paul's day because of their exaltation of the law. But such is the human heart, and so great is the temptation of people in every age and race to deceive themselves into thinking that their lives are good enough for God, that the reminder of this verse is needed still. If this salvation is of God's grace and received simply through faith, it is *not because of works* (Rom. 3:20, 28; 4:1–5; Gal. 2:16; 2 Tim. 1:9; Tit. 3:5). For 'all have sinned' (Rom. 3:23), and suffer sin's consequences, exclusion from life in fellowship with God. This means furthermore that no-one can *boast* before God, since all are admitted on the grounds of grace. 'Some room', says Calvin, 'must always remain for man's boasting, so long as, independently of grace, merits are of any avail.' But merits have no place. God will allow no-one to boast (*cf.* Rom. 3:27). The words here may in fact imply that this was a part of God's purpose and the reason for his bringing salvation as he did, to exclude human pride (*cf.* Jdg. 7:2). Or perhaps we should take it simply as a result, 'There is

[1]C. Brown, *St. Paul's Epistle to the Ephesians: A Devotional Commentary* (London, 1911), p. 48.

nothing for anyone to boast of' (NEB). In either case it is made clear that the only right attitude, the only possible attitude for sinful men and women before their Maker and their Judge is penitence and humble dependence. Their only pride can be in the cross by which they find salvation (Gal. 6:14) and the Saviour who suffered there (1 Cor. 1:29–31; Phil. 3:3ff.).

10. The work of God in Christ has been described as the gift of new life, and as the gift of salvation. Now it is shown further that people of themselves could not accomplish it by its being described as God's new creation. We, in this new life, this new nature that we have received, are *his workmanship*. The Greek again gains emphasis by the word order, as it makes the *his* stand first in the sentence. The noun used (*poiēma*) is from a different root to the 'works' (*ergon*) of the previous verse, and is found elsewhere in the New Testament only in Romans 1:20, where it is used of the works of God's first creation. Humanity was his making at the first, and now, because that work of his was spoilt by sin, there is a new divine act of creation. For 'if any one is in Christ, he is a new creation' (2 Cor. 5:17; see also Eph. 4:24; Gal. 6:15; Col. 3:10). *In Christ Jesus* – the phrase comes for the third time in five verses – in faith-union with him, those whose lives were marred and ruined by failure and sin are made new.

'Works' have been excluded as a means of amassing merit and gaining favour with God. The gulf between God and sinful humanity must be bridged by God's action. The new life in fellowship with God must be God's creation and cannot be our work. But nevertheless the essential quality of the new life is *good works*. The preposition here (Gk. *epi*, AV 'unto', RV and RSV *for*) shows that more is involved than saying that good works were the purpose of the new life, or that people were redeemed in order to be a people 'zealous for good deeds' (Tit. 2:14; *cf.* Col. 1:10); rather it is that good works are 'involved' in the new life 'as an inseparable condition' (Abbott). His new creation must be spoken of as being 'in true righteousness and holiness' (Eph. 4:24). It is of such a kind that it must and will express itself in this way.

To demonstrate this still further as being the divine purpose Paul adds concerning such good works that *God* has *prepared beforehand, that we should walk in them.* This does not of necessity mean that there are particular good works that are God's purpose for us. There can be no objection to such a concept, if it is reckoned that the foreknowledge of an almighty and omniscient God is not opposed to his gift of free will. But probably it is rather the whole course of life that is on view here. The nature and character of the works and the direction of the Christian's daily *walk* (see on 2:2) are predetermined. This then corresponds closely with 1:4 which describes the end and goal of election as 'that we should be holy and blameless before him'. R. W. Dale puts it, 'As the branch is created in the vine, we are created in Christ; as the fruits of the branch are predetermined by the laws of that life which it receives from the vine, so our "good works" which are the result of our union with Christ, are predetermined by the laws of the life of Christ which is our life. . . .'

B. THE RECONCILIATION OF JEWS AND GENTILES (2:11–22)

11. The purpose of Christ's work for human salvation is not limited to the giving of new life to individual men and women, previously dead in sin, as the last section has described. Chapter 1 has given hints that it goes beyond this, and the present section now shows that it involves the bringing of those individuals, whatever their race or background, into unity in the people of God. In this respect it involves the greatest transformation of situation for the Gentiles, and this section, like verses 1–10, begins by showing what was the condition of Gentiles in the past. As John Stott puts it we have 'the portrait of an alienated humanity', then, 'the portrait of the peace-making Christ' and lastly 'the portrait of God's new society'. Paul's readers are called to *remember* and thus be stirred to love and gratitude. Firstly, they should think of the great change that has come in their relationship with the Jews, their connection with those who were named the people of God. Just as the Greeks despised those who lived outside of their cities, calling them *ethnē* (pagans), so the Jews in their superficial and unspiritual way of thinking (*in the flesh*), instead of regarding the other nations as those with whom they should have shared their knowledge of God (*cf.* Gn. 12:3; Is. 42:1, 6; 49:6), simply spoke disparagingly of them as *Gentiles* (*ethnē*).[1] They called them *the uncircumcision*, those who did not have on them the mark of the covenant of God with his people. This was the proud judgment of those who called themselves *the circumcision*, although from the standpoint of one in Christ this mark might be only *made in the flesh by hands*.

Elsewhere in the Pauline letters we find this contrast between the circumcision which is of the Spirit and that which is merely of the flesh, a work of human hands; and we may compare the way the same term is used in the New Testament to describe the tabernacle and temple (Mk. 14:58; Acts 7:48; Heb. 9:11, 24) when contrasted with the spiritual temple as Paul speaks of it here in verse 21. Paul did not disparage circumcision as an institution. It was to him the God-given sign of the covenant; but if the outward sign was not matched by an inward faith and an obedience of life to the covenant, it became worthless and just a work of the flesh (1 Cor. 7:19; Gal. 5:6; 6:15). The circumcision that mattered, whether or not there was any outward sign, was spiritual circumcision, a putting off of sin and an obedience to Christ (Rom. 2:25–29; Phil. 3:2–3; Col. 2:11).

12. The fundamental change for the Gentiles, however, was not simply in the way that the Jews regarded them, but in their actual condition. Their lack of privilege and opportunity might be described in the far-reaching terms of this verse. *At that time,* before they came to know and experience the grace of God, they were *separated from Christ.* These words may stand as the first description of the position of the Gentiles (as RSV puts its), or, perhaps, as the basic one on which the others depend (AV). In the latter case we may see this whole section as drawing out the contrast between what the Gentiles were without the hope of the Messiah, and all that went with that, and what they came to be 'in Christ Jesus' (v. 13).

They were *alienated from the commonwealth of Israel.* They did not belong to, and found themselves cut off from, the fellowship and the privileges (such as Rom. 3:1–2 and 9:4–5 describe) of

[1]Barclay, p. 125, well illustrates the extreme forms that the Jewish contempt for Gentiles could take.

those who truly called themselves the people of God. The word used for *alienated* is that used in 4:18 and Colossians 1:21 for humanity's separation from God by sin. The only other New Testament use of the word translated *commonwealth* is in Acts 22:28, where it refers to the much-coveted Roman citizenship. Whatever purpose of God for the Gentiles may have been expressed in the Old Testament, in actual fact they stood almost entirely outside the spiritual privileges of Israel. The Jews did admit Gentiles as proselytes, it is true, but the way of entry was difficult, and even then the sense of alienation was not fully removed. At least by birth Gentiles were *strangers to the covenants of promise.* The promise to the Jews, *the* promise of the Messiah (Gk. has the article), was involved in the covenants with Abraham and the patriarchs (Gn. 17:1–14; 26:24; 28:13–15), and with the nation under Moses (Ex. 24:1–11). The covenants brought Israel into a special relationship of grace with God, and so to the hope of a deliverance and future glory that would be theirs. But up till this time the Gentiles had not been included within these covenants. So they stood as a people with *no hope.*

In fact they were not only without the hope that Israel had, but they were without any real hope at all. This was a very evident characteristic of the Gentile world of the time when Jesus came. People had no prospect for the future, no assurance of life beyond this. The Greeks, for example, looked back on a golden age in the past rather than to a future glory; or more philosophically they took a cyclic view of history. There was in consequence no concept of a goal to which all things were moving, and this lack of hope was seen most notably in their view of death.

Finally, Paul says that they were *without God.* the Greek word here (*atheoi*) does not mean that they refused to believe in God, or that they were forsaken by God, or godless in their conduct, but that they had no real knowledge of God. In most cases they had many objects of worship – 'many "gods" and many "lords" ' – but they were gods in name only (1 Cor. 8:4–5; Gal. 4:8). Some sought for the One in philosophy; some tried to come within the fold of Judaism; but by and large the Gentiles had to live *in the world* lives limited by the things of the world, and had to face the trials and sorrows and perplexities of the world without the knowledge of God to interpret the whole.

13. Now, however, for these Gentiles, everything had become different, because from being 'separated from Christ' (v. 12), they had come to be *in Christ Jesus.* They had come to find their life in him. They who had been *far off* – far from God, and with a great gulf dividing them from his covenant people – were *brought near.* The Rabbis had a way of speaking of Gentiles, who were far from the privileges of the covenant, as being 'brought near' as proselytes.[1] But Paul is speaking of a far more fundamental and wonderful way of approach by *the blood of Christ* (see on 1:7). For the basic cause of human estrangement is sin, and Christ gave himself as a sacrifice for the sins of the whole world (Jn. 3:16; 12:32; 2 Cor. 5:19; 1 Jn. 2:2). The sins of both Jews and Gentiles can be forgiven because of his death, and both can be *brought near* to God as never before, and so *brought near* to each other. Divisions are overcome, not by an approaching or a receiving on either side, but by Christ coming and making peace for both.

14. Not only can it be said that Christ brings peace. *He is our peace.* As men and women are brought to be in him, and continue to live in him, they find peace with God, and so also a meeting-place and concord with one another, whatever may have been their divisions of race, colour, class or creed before. He came for this purpose (Lk. 2:14), to be the Prince of peace, and indeed in such terms the prophets had foretold his coming (Is. 9:6–7; 53:5; Mi. 5:5; Hg. 2:9; Zc. 9:10). By his coming and supremely by his cross, he *has made us both one.* The Greek says literally that 'he has made both things into one thing' (later, in v. 15, the personal is used). The organization of Judaism and that of the Gentile world no longer stand apart as before. Divisions and distinctions no longer exist as far as the standing of any before God is concerned. God has made a way for the divided to become one (*cf.* Jn. 10:16; 17:11; 1 Cor. 10:17; 12:13).

Paul is pre-occupied, however, with what to him was the

---

[1]See quotations from the rabbinical writings in Abbott, p. 60.

greatest division of all, that which separated Jews and Gentiles. There had always been a *dividing wall of hostility* between the two. There was a barrier both literally and spiritually. In Jerusalem, between the temple proper and the Court of the Gentiles, there was a stone wall on which there was an inscription in Greek and Latin: 'No one of another nation to enter within the fence and enclosure round the temple. And whoever is caught will have himself to blame that his death ensues.'[1] It is strangely significant that Paul was finally arrested and condemned by the Jews in Jerusalem on the basis of a false accusation that he took an Ephesian, Trophimus, beyond this barrier (Acts 21:29–30). But Christ had now *broken down* the barrier between Jews and Gentiles, of which that dividing wall in the temple was a symbol.

15. In order, however, that that particular dividing wall between Jews and Gentiles might be broken down, two things closely connected in the minds of strict Jews had to be dealt with. The old 'hostility' (v. 14) had to go. The feeling of animosity and hostility had to be replaced by a sense of fellowship. Secondly, *the law of commandments and ordinances* had to be abolished (*cf.* Col. 2:14, 20). The law with its detailed ordinances of ceremonies and regulations about the clean and the unclean had the effect of imposing a barrier and of causing enmity between Jews and Gentiles. Indeed also the moral law broken by all people left all condemned and alienated. 'Jesus abolished both the regulations of the ceremonial law and the condemnation of the moral law' (Stott).

Because Christ has come and by what he has done *in his flesh*, especially by his death (see Col. 1:22), salvation and acceptance with God in his people is offered to all people on condition of repentance and faith. Peter was sent to Cornelius and bidden to regard no longer the distinction between ceremonial cleanness and uncleanness (Acts 10). The church in its council at Jerusalem had agreed that there was no longer to be a barrier because the Jews had circumcision and all the other ordinances of the law,

[1]Josephus in his *Antiquities* xv.11.5 and *The Wars of the Jews* v.5.2; vi.2.4 tells us of this, and such an inscription was discovered by the French archaeologist M. Clermont Ganneau in 1871, and another, now in the Rockefeller Museum in Jerusalem, was discovered in 1934.

and the Gentiles did not (Acts 15). The Lord came not to destroy
the law, but to fulfil it (Mt. 5:17). Much of the law (*e.g.* the
sacrificial ritual) was preparation for, and foreshadowing of, the
Christ, and so was fulfilled by what he did when he came. The
moral demands and principles of the law were not lightened by
Jesus, but made fuller and more far-reaching (Mt. 5:21–48). In
the discipline of obedience that its detailed regulations
demanded, and as the revealer of right and wrong, it was
intended to lead to Christ (Gal. 3:24). In an absolute sense it
cannot be said to be made of no effect in Christ (Rom. 3:31). But
as a code 'specific, rigid, and outward, fulfilled in external
ordinances' (Westcott), and so serving to separate Jews and
Gentiles, it was abolished (*cf.* Col. 2:20–22).

The Lord's coming meant *making peace* between Jew and Gentile, by taking away the cause of division. The law could no
longer be the way by which Jews, and Jews alone, could try to
come to God. The way of approach is now by grace, by a new
creative work of God, the same for both Jews and Gentiles. The
purpose of Christ is 'to create out of the two a single new
humanity in himself' (NEB). *In* Christ there is a new humanity;
and it is a single entity. God now deals with Jews and Gentiles
as such a single entity. Furthermore, Gentiles do not simply rise
to the status of Jews, but both become something *new* and
greater; and it is significant that the word for *new* here *(kainos)*
means not simply new in point of time, but as Barclay puts it
'new in the sense that it brings into the world a new kind of
thing, a new quality of thing, which did not exist before' (see
also on 4:23–24).

16. Right through this passage the twin themes of the reconciliation to God, and of people to one another, are inextricably
intertwined. *Through the cross* the purpose of Christ was to
reconcile people *to God* (*cf.* Rom. 5:10; 2 Cor. 5:18–20; Col. 1:20).
When he was slain there *the hostility* between humanity and God
through sin was brought to an end, because he bore our sins
and made possible our forgiveness. He thus reconciled *both* Jew
and Gentile *to God*, but he also reconciled them (and the people
of all the different divisions of mankind) to one another and
brought them to be *in one body*, thus putting to death *the hostility*

91

between them. What he has done once and for all 'in his body of flesh by his death' (Col. 1:22), he now effects in the *one body* which is his church. But here we should note that the emphasis is not quite that of 1:23 on the church as Christ's body, but rather on the fact that there is one living organism in which members so diverse belong together (*cf.* 4:4; 1 Cor. 10:17; 12:13; Col. 3:15).

17–18. The same linking of the thought of the new relationship to God and to one's fellows continues in these next two verses. The coming of Christ meant that *peace* could be *preached* to them *who were far off*, the Gentiles, who previously had 'no hope' and were 'without God in the world' (v. 12), and *to those who were near*, the Jews, who had 'the covenants of promise' (v. 12) and belonged to the people of God (*cf.* Dt. 4:7; Ps. 148:14). For both this was peace with God, which both equally needed; and its consequence was peace and concord one with the other as well. In the words of this verse there is an allusion (as perhaps also in v. 13) to Isaiah 57:19, and probably also to Isaiah 52:7 which speaks of the preaching of peace. These Old Testament passages (referred to also in Acts 2:39 and Rom. 10:15) did not originally speak of the way of peace for the Gentiles, but such words of Scripture, deeply imprinted on the apostle's mind, found an apt application to this wonderful new situation. The form of expression, thus dependent on the Old Testament words, is not to be pressed too far. We are not to ask what preaching of the gospel of peace this refers to – before or after the resurrection, before or after Pentecost. The point is that Christ came 'with a gospel of peace' (Moffatt). Through his cross peace was made, and he through his church takes out the message of reconciliation and peace to the world (*cf.* Acts 10:36; 2 Cor. 5:18–20).

Then further, the apostle says, *through him*, Jesus Christ, *we both have access . . . to the Father*. *Access* is probably the best translation of *prosagōgē*, though it could be 'introduction'. In oriental courts there was a *prosagōgeus* who brought a person into the presence of the king. The thought could be of Christ as the *prosagōgeus*, but the form of expression in the whole clause suggests rather that by him there is a way of approach (*cf.* 3:12).

He is the door, the way to the Father (Jn. 10:7, 9; 14:6); by him men and women, though sinners, because they are reconciled can 'with confidence draw near to the throne of grace' (Heb. 4:16). But it is added that the *access* is for *both* Jew and Gentile *in one Spirit* (*cf.* 1 Cor. 12:13). There is one way for all, *one Spirit* by whose work in their hearts they have assurance that they can come to God as children to a Father (Rom. 8:15–16; Gal. 4:6). The personal Spirit of God is obviously intended here, and the form of the phrase should be noted. As Paul repeatedly uses the words 'in Christ' in this letter, so a number of times he says 'in the Spirit', to emphasize that for the new life of the Christian 'the Spirit is, as it were, the surrounding, sustaining power' (Westcott).

19. The unity of all Christians 'in one Spirit' will find emphasis and development in chapter 4, but now the apostle turns back specifically to the Gentiles to speak further of the change in their status and position. Before they were 'alienated from the commonwealth of Israel' (v. 12). In relation to the covenant people of God, they were *strangers and sojourners* (*xenoi* and *paroikoi*), that is, people who might live alongside them in the same country, but owning no land and with only the most superficial rights of citizenship. Such was their old position, but it is so *no longer*. Now, the apostle says, *you are fellow citizens with the saints.* His mind might have gone to the *saints* of Old Testament times, or to members of the Christian church to all of whom the word applied (see on 1:1); probably he thought of all who in any sense could be called the people of God, and so he said to the Gentiles that they were now included among them, and on equal terms.

Citizenship of the people of God was one expressive way of telling the truth concerning the position in God's kingdom that Jews and Gentiles now equally share. But this description had to give way to one that connoted a further truth, and could speak of the greater intimacy that Christians have with God, and indeed with one another. Jews and Gentiles, people of whatever race or colour or class, are together *of the household of God*, of the same family. Galatians 6:10 uses the same word *oikeioi*, speaking of 'the household of faith'. Although the word does not fully

93

express the truth that all are children of God by faith in Christ Jesus (Gal. 3:26; and see on 1:5), yet the thought is of the people of the household rather than the building (*cf.* Heb. 3:2, 5–6; 1 Pet. 4:17).

20. In what follows now, however, there are truths that can be contained best by the description of the house (*oikos*) as a building. Those whose faith is in Christ Jesus are like an edifice *built* (*epoikodomēthentes*) *upon the foundation of the apostles and prophets.* The question is asked whether this does not go against the Pauline picture of the house in 1 Corinthians 3:11, where it is said that 'There can be no other foundation beyond that which is already laid; . . . Jesus Christ himself' (NEB). To overcome the assumed difficulty some have suggested that we should take the words here to mean the foundation that they laid in the lives of others, or that they had built on in their work. We need not feel that this is necessary. What we have here we may regard simply as a slightly different handling of the same metaphor as that in 1 Corinthians 3. (*Cf.* Rev. 21:14 for a use that is different again but not contradictory.) There the apostle thought of himself and others as builders, here as stones in the building. As Allan puts it, 'The Church rests on the total unique Event of which Christ is the centre, but in which the apostles and prophets, filled and guided by the Spirit and doing their work in unique closeness to Christ, had an indispensable and untransmissible part.' To *apostles and prophets* the word of God in Christ was revealed in a unique way (*cf.* 3:5). Because they received, believed and witnessed to that word, they were the beginning of the building on which others were to be built (*cf.* Mt. 16:16–18). That the prophets of the Christian church and not of the Old Testament are intended here is clear from the order of the phrase *apostles and prophets*, and by the way that both words come under the same definite article in the Greek.[1] (Note the use of the same phrase in 3:5, and for the work of these Christian prophets see on 4:11.)

As the building metaphor is applied here *Christ Jesus himself* is

---

[1] W. Grudem in *The Gift of Prophecy in 1 Corinthians* (University Press of America, Lanham, MA, 1982), pp. 90–105, has argued that the phrase here and in 3:5 should be translated 'the apostles who are also prophets'; while this is possible, two separate categories of 'apostles' and 'prophets' are clearly in view in 4:11.

described as *the cornerstone*. This thought comes from Psalm 118:22, a passage which was used by our Lord himself (Mk. 12:10), and then in the early church, 'The very stone which the builders rejected has become the head of the corner' (1 Pet. 2:7; see also Acts 4:11). It denotes primarily the honour of his position in the building, but then also the way in which each stone is fitted into him, and finds its true place and usefulness only in relation to him (*cf.* Col. 2:7; 1 Pet. 2:4–5). There is some difference of opinion as to the precise place of the cornerstone in the building, but it seems most likely that it was the stone set in the foundations at the corner to bind all together and to give the walls their line.[1] Isaiah 28:16, which is quoted together with Psalm 118:22 in 1 Peter 2, speaks of the stone laid in Zion as 'a precious cornerstone, of a sure foundation'. The significance of Christ described in this way removes any possible thought of the Lord himself as the foundation being replaced by the apostles.

21–22. Whatever the precise position of the cornerstone the main point of the metaphor is made explicit when it is said now that in Christ all that is built into the edifice *is joined together*. All find their true place and function in relation to Christ and as they are built into him. *The whole structure* does not appear strictly correct as a translation, since there is no article in the original. A more accurate translation would be 'every building' or 'each several building' (RV); but while this is a more exact rendering it is hardly true to the apostle's thought to suggest that the church is like a number of different buildings. The word use (*oikodomē*) has a wide range of meaning. It is used sometimes for individual buildings (*e.g.* in Mk. 13:1–2), but very often in the New Testament for the whole work of building, and hence in the spiritual sense of 'building', of 'edification' (as in 4:12, 16, 29). It is the whole operation of building that is in view here (and probably similarly in 1 Cor. 3:9), as the present participle being *joined together*, and then the verb that follows, indicate. So we may say 'everything that is being built', or as Phillips puts it 'each separate piece of building'.

The work is developing; the church cannot be described as a

[1] The idea of the stone being the keystone at the top of an arch locking the whole structure together is less likely since this building 'is not yet completed' (Mitton, *NCB*).

95

complete edifice until the final day of the Lord comes (*cf.* Rev. 21). It is growing towards what it is intended to be in the purpose of God. The metaphor is inadequate at this point. There must be the thought of organic growth; the stones are 'living stones' (1 Pet. 2:5). To express this the description of the church as a living body is preferable (as in 4:15–16). But the metaphor of the building has not been exhausted, and what is probably the chief reason for its use has not yet been expressed. There is an analogy that can be drawn from the Old Testament that conveys a deep truth; this building *grows into a holy temple*. We see the truth as we note the actual word used. It is not the general word (*hieron*) that described the whole of the temple precincts, but that used for the inner shrine (*naos*). The temple in Old Testament days, and especially considered as *naos*, was above all else the special meeting-place between God and his people. It was the place on which the glory of God descended, the place of his presence. When Christ came, he made obsolete the tabernacle or temple made with hands. He himself was the place of the divine dwelling among men, a truth that is expressed particularly in John 1:14 and 2:19–21. That temple is no longer among us, but now God seeks as his *dwelling place* the lives of men and women who will allow him to enter by his Spirit.

Two further points are to be noted about the apostle's thought here. Firstly, verse 21 ends with the words *in the Lord*, and verse 22 with *in the Spirit* to emphasize yet again that it is only by a person being in Christ, in the Spirit (see on 2:18), that the work of building into the habitation of God can take place. Abiding in Christ and Christ in his people belong inextricably together (*cf.* Jn. 15:4–7). None can have any true place in the eternal building of God, unless they have found life in Christ. Secondly, we are reminded how far removed the New Testament thought is from our individualistic concepts. In 1 Corinthians 6:19 Paul does speak of the individual Christian's body as the 'temple [*naos*] of the Holy Spirit', but his thought dwells rather on the community of Christians as the temple (2 Cor. 6:16), or as one organism indwelt by the living Christ. It is true that unity is not a matter of organization, but of the sharing of the common life and tasks of the body, but it behoves all Christians to take warning of the danger of individualistic Christian service, and to consider seriously the things that hinder the expression of that common life and the united fulfilling of the tasks. In Philippians 2:1–3 and 4:2 Paul had to speak against divisions due to personal rivalries, and in 1 Corinthians 1 and 3 against the danger of breaking up into sects for the sake of loyalty to honoured leaders rather than to Christ. Here he has had in mind the Jewish-Gentile animosities that in earlier days threatened to make two churches instead of one, and now to Gentile Christians he says – what many Jewish Christians before had been loath to accept – *you also are built* together *into* this *holy temple,* this *dwelling place of God in the Spirit.*

C. THE PRIVILEGE OF PROCLAMATION (3:1–13)

1. There is a pattern of development in these first three chapters of the letter. In chapter 1 the apostle's meditation on the wealth of the blessings of God in Christ has led naturally to prayer. In chapter 2 he has developed further his great theme of the purpose of God in Christ, as he has spoken of the amazing grace of God in bringing those dead in sin to new life in Christ, and of the far-reaching significance of the reconciling of Jew and Gentile together in the one people of God. His expression of these great facts, which have a practical importance that touches the whole of life, leads him naturally to prayer again. So he begins *For this reason* (*cf.* 1:15) and he is about to add 'I bow my knees' (v. 14), but deeply aware of his position and the nature of his relationship with those to whom he writes, and for whom he would pray, he says, *I, Paul, a prisoner for Christ Jesus on behalf of you Gentiles,* and this leads him away from his prayer for a moment.

As we saw in the beginning (on 1:1) Paul's apostleship determined all his life, the work that he did, and the nature of his relationships with people. Paul could never fail to be conscious of it, as he wrote, and as he prayed. The repeated *I Paul* of his letters shows this (2 Cor. 10:1; Gal. 5:2; Col. 1:23; 1 Thes. 2:18; Phm. 19). Now in particular 'he hears as it were the clink of his chain, and remembers where he is and why he is there' (Robinson). Because he was the apostle of the Gentiles, and very directly as a result of his stand for the equality of Jews and

Gentiles in the people of God (see Acts 21:17–34; 22:21–24; 26:12–23) he was in prison. For the sake of the Gentiles he had been imprisoned, and even now his confinement was to their advantage (v. 13). He writes like this not because he was dispirited or disappointed. He wanted no pity and would allow no-one to be dejected because of his imprisonment. He saw it in a light which burnt out all self-pity. To outward appearance he was the prisoner of Rome, confined by the will of men. But just as his spiritual life 'in Christ' mattered far more to him than his outward circumstances and environment, so now he regarded himself as a prisoner by the will of his master. Therefore (translating more literally than RSV) he could gladly call himself 'the prisoner of Christ Jesus' (cf. 4:1; 2 Tim. 1:8; Phm. 1, 9); just as for every part of his life he could call himself the slave of Christ (e.g. Phil. 1:1).

2. His speaking like this led him, before he continued with his prayer, to dwell on his calling as the apostle to the Gentiles, and on what it meant to him. To him had been entrusted a *stewardship of God's grace* with particular reference to the Gentiles. We considered this word here translated *stewardship* when it occurred in 1:10, and we found that it meant basically either the administration of a household, or the office of the one who administered it. Paul here is thinking especially of the stewardship entrusted to him (cf. 1 Cor. 4:1; 9:17), though the other thought of the arrangement or purpose of God is not far away. Colossians 1:25 is a close parallel, and the thought is also that of Galatians 2:7 where Paul says how 'the gospel to the uncircumcised' was entrusted to him as that 'to the circumcised' was to Peter.

To express this trust that he has he uses the word *grace. Grace* is used in its fullest and widest sense of the undeserved favour of God that brings to men and women all that they need for living a Christian life (Acts 13:43; 14:26; 2 Cor. 9:8). But Paul also uses it a number of times to express the privilege of being given a work to do for Christ, and to denote the particular task allotted in his service (cf. Rom. 12:3, 6; Eph. 4:7). In his own case it was the amazing favour of being called to be an apostle (Rom. 15:15–16; 1 Cor. 3:10; Gal. 2:9) and that to the Gentiles. There is yet another application of the word that is found in Acts 11:23, and that rings through this whole section, that in the actual extension of the privileges of the gospel to the Gentiles the particular mercy of God has been shown. There is grace to the Gentiles that apostles of the gospel were sent to them, and grace to Paul that he should be their apostle; the two thoughts are intertwined in the use of the word *grace* in this section.

Paul feels it necessary, however, to press on his readers the fact that he has been entrusted with this grace and responsibility; and we have seen that this is a strong argument for the view that this letter was sent originally not to the Christians at Ephesus alone, but to a wider circle.[1] The Greek particle *ei ge* that begins this verse does not express doubt (as AV and RV imply) but it calls on the readers to verify what is being said (*cf.* its use in 4:21; 2 Cor. 5:3; Gal. 3:4; Col. 1:23). So RSV translates *assuming that you have heard*, and NEB 'for surely you have heard . . .'. The argument concerning the destination still applies, however, as even this is hardly what he would say to a church that knew him as well as did the church at Ephesus, but rather to those of whom some, as least, knew him only 'by reputation' (Scott).

3. If they appreciated the way that a special knowledge of the purpose of God for the Gentiles had been given to him, and of the particular part in the working out of that purpose that was entrusted to him, they would agree that *by revelation* God had *made known* to him *the mystery*. From 1:9 we have seen that 'revealing' and 'making known' go naturally with the word *mystery* when it is used in connection with the gospel. For this is the truth of God which is no longer hidden, but made plain to those who are willing to receive it. To Paul it had been a revelation in a special sense. Previously he had been a strict Jew of the exclusive party of the Pharisees, and it took a clear revelation from God to convince him. Moreover, at that time, the earlier apostles were not sufficiently clear and unequivocal in their stand on the equality of the Gentiles in the people of God, and so from that standpoint also a revelation was necessary, as Paul shows in Galatians 1 – 2. Here he is concerned to tell not how the communication came to him, but rather the content of it. He has

[1]See pp. 22–24.

expressed this – the inclusion of the Gentiles with the Jews in the one body and household – and it is to what he has said already in this letter, not to some earlier letter, that he refers when he says, using what the grammarians call an epistolary aorist: *as I have written briefly*. This epistolary aorist (*cf.* 1 Pet. 5:12) is better translated as in the NEB, 'I have already written a brief account of this'.

4. It has been suggested that *when you read* could refer to the reading of the Old Testament (RSV *this* is not in the original), as supporting Paul's understanding of the purpose of God for the Gentiles. Matthew 24:15 is compared to indicate that such a way of speaking could have reference to the Old Testament. But nowhere else in the New Testament is the Old so referred to without some specific mention of it. It is much more natural to take it as meaning that when they read what he had already 'written briefly' (v. 3), they will *perceive his insight into the mystery of Christ*. Nor need we suppose that if this is the meaning, it shows in Paul a spirit of personal pride and boasting, or leads us to doubt the authenticity of the letter. We have considered this in dealing with the question of authorship in the Introduction. The point is that in this context, as repeatedly elsewhere, Paul is at pains to emphasize that all his understanding is by the gift of God, and only possible as he reveals his truth. The knowledge of *the mystery* was not a personal discovery upon which he could flatter himself. It was the gift of God by his Spirit (*cf.* 1:8–9, 17–18). He may pride himself in his knowledge, as he does in 2 Corinthians 11:5–6, but he realizes and states that it is only by God-given enlightenment that he possesses the truth. Moreover his purpose is not self-glorification but to help people recognize the word of God in his teaching, and thus accept its authority.

At this point we should look also into another difficulty felt in this section. What is the meaning of *the mystery of Christ* here? In particular, is it defined in a way that is different from its definition in Colossians? It has been asserted that the difference is so great as to make common authorship impossible.[1] In Colossians 1:27 it is stated specifically that the mystery is 'Christ in you, the

[1]See pp. 28.

hope of glory', that is to say, the actual mystery, the wonderful truth that has been revealed, is that Christ comes to dwell now in people's hearts, giving them hope of a future in the immediate presence of God. In verse 6 of this chapter the mystery seems to be taken equally specifically as 'how the Gentiles are fellow heirs, ... partakers of the promise in Christ Jesus through the gospel'. Are these two incompatible in the same writer? Can they not be different aspects of the central revelation? In Colossians 2:2 the mystery is simply 'Christ', and indeed it is possible to take the genitive as meaning that here. In this same letter (in Eph. 1:9–10) it should be noted that Paul can speak of the mystery without any specific reference to the Gentiles; there it is the purpose of God to 'gather together in one all things in Christ' (AV). It therefore seems unnecessary to regard the meaning of *the mystery* in Ephesians and Colossians as being contradictory. It seems easier to say that Paul thought of *the mystery* as the great purpose of God in Christ. His mind dwelt now on one aspect of it, now on another; even in the same letter there are slight differences in the use of the word. As Bruce (*NICNT*) puts it, he could refer to 'one particular element of his message' as *the mystery*, or to the message as a whole. Identity of authorship need not be questioned on the ground of such differences.

5. In Romans 16:25–26 Paul speaks of the mystery (which there connotes the full gospel of Christ) as 'kept secret for long ages but . . . now disclosed'. In Colossians 1:26, which is closely parallel to this section, he speaks of it as 'hidden for ages and generations but now made manifest to his saints'. Here he says the same thing in particular about the bringing in of the Gentiles. This is not to deny that there were glimpses of God's purpose in this matter in the Old Testament (as in such passages as the apostle quotes in Rom. 15:9–12); but it is a truth that had not been at all fully understood that Jews and Gentiles should actually become one people, and it certainly had not been carried into practical effect. It *was not made known to the sons of men in other generations as it has now been revealed*; and we may take the force of the 'as' to mean 'in such measure as' or 'with such clarity as' now. In particular its reality 'had burst upon Paul with all the amazement of a new revelation' (Caird).

To *apostles and prophets* (the prophets of the new order, as we have seen on 2:20)[1], *the Spirit* has been at pains to reveal this. (The phrase, lit. 'in the Spirit', discussed on 2:18 and 22, is repeated here.) The Acts of the Apostles (10:9–20; 11:4–12; 15:7–9) records how the Spirit gave the revelation of this truth to Peter, and we have recalled the way in which Galatians (1:15–16; 2:1–9) tells the manner of the revelation to Paul. As we have seen,[2] the phrase *holy apostles* is not to be considered strange, a mark of pride on the lips of an apostle, or otherwise evidence that it was not written by an apostle. *Holy* (*hagios*, see on 1:1) has not the connotation in the New Testament that it has in modern English. Paul, without any vain-glory, could use in relation to himself both words, 'holy' and 'apostle'.

6. Paul has spoken of the way that the Jews regarded the Gentiles (2:11), and indeed of the way in which they actually stood in relation to the people of God (2:12ff.). He himself had been a proud Pharisee, and shared the general Jewish disparagement of the Gentiles. His conversion meant a complete transformation in his thinking. He was turned to see Jesus, whom he had persecuted, as the Christ, the Son of God, and the only saviour. His whole attitude to the Gentiles was also revolutionized in this same crisis of this experience. By revelation he came to see that Jews and Gentiles can now stand together in the people of God. They are *fellow heirs*, they share the same inheritance in the heavenly riches of God (1:11–14; Gal. 3:29; 4:7). They are *of the same body*. One word (*synsōma*) is used for this in the Greek; it is not known in Greek literature before Paul, and perhaps was coined by him to express this truth that the Gentiles are incorporated with Jews in the one body of Christ (*cf.* 2:16). They are also *partakers of the promise* – they share on equal terms with Jews the promise of life and salvation (*cf.* 2 Tim. 1:1), though before the Gentiles were 'strangers to the covenants of promise' (Eph. 2:12). All of these privileges they can share with the Jews because, in the same way as they, the Gentiles can now find their life *in Christ Jesus through the gospel. The gospel*, as it is

[1]But see Grudem, *Gift of Prophecy*, pp. 90–105.   [2]See p. 39.

preached and believed, is the effectual means, humanly speaking, by which men and women come to be *in Christ*. (*Cf.* the use of the same phrase in 1 Cor. 4:15.) That gospel, therefore, is the means and the only means of deep spiritual unity between people, however diverse their racial, cultural or political backgrounds.

7. Because of this fact Paul cannot do other than speak exultantly of the privilege and responsibility and significance of his being made *a minister* of that gospel (*cf.* Gal. 1:13–16; Col. 1:23–29; 1 Tim. 1:12–16). The Greek word here (*diakonos*) is used sometimes in the New Testament of those of a particular office (Phil. 1:1; 1 Tim. 3:8–12); but it is often used more generally of one who lived and worked in the service (*diakonia*, as in 4:12) of Christ. (See 6:21 and 2 Cor. 3:6; 11:23; Col. 1:23; 1 Tim. 4:6.) Paul gladly accepted the title of servant, but he realized his utter inadequacy in himself to fulfil the responsibility that it laid on him to communicate to others the word and good news of God (*cf.* 2 Cor. 3:5; 4:1; 12:9–10). Only by a twofold gift from God was it possible for him to be such. He was *a minister according to the gift of God's grace* and *by the working of his power*. Verse 2 has spoken in the same terms of the gift of *God's grace* and there we have seen the range of the use of this word 'grace' in the New Testament and in particular in Paul's writings. He was unworthy to be a preacher of God's word, because he had been a persecutor; but the grace of God had made him all that he was, a new man in Christ (1 Cor. 15:10). It also made him Christ's servant in the proclamation of his *gospel*, and in the particular work that he had of ministering it to the Gentiles. But mercy was not enough. He was also *a minister . . . by the working of his power*. The task to which he was called needed no mere human strength and patience and power of endurance. It needed the power of God and, as in 1:19, Paul shows that that power is given, and not just as an abstract thing, or as a force applied from afar, but as ener-gizing strength (*energeia*) operative in his life by the Spirit's indwelling. In Colossians 1:29 he expresses this more fully when he says of his preaching work, 'I toil, striving with all the energy which he mightily inspires within me'. By the grace of

God he was called and received as a servant of the gospel, and by the power of God he did all that was effective in that service.

8. Paul cannot stop with what he has said, but must dwell further on the incredible grace of God and on his personal unworthiness. He was 'less than the least of all saints'. So AV translates more literally than RSV as the apostle invents a comparative of a superlative to express himself more forcefully.[1] This is no feigned humility. It is the inevitable attitude of one who was prostrated with wonder at the grace of God in Christ. Here it is not so much that he is consciously comparing himself with others; if he did so he might speak as he does in 2 Corinthians 12:11. Nor is it because he had specially in mind the fact that he had been a persecutor (as in 1 Cor. 15:9; Gal. 1:13–15; 1 Tim. 1:12–14). Rather it is that the more he meditated on the blessings of God in Christ, and the infinite grace of his gifts, the more he realized that in himself there was nothing to make him deserve such mercy. He knew that he had no standing, no personal worthiness, no claim, no natural position or gifts, that he should receive the grace of reconciliation, and become a preacher of it. He was *the very least of all*. The gospel was everything, *the unsearchable riches of Christ*.

We have seen already the apostle's love for terms that speak of wealth to express the blessings of Christ that infinitely transcend the world's riches (see on 1:7). Here he adds an adjective (*anexichniaston*) that speaks of something that cannot be traced out by human footprints. It is used of the works of God in the Septuagint of Job 5:9 and 9:10. If Paul tried to measure and define that grace, he would find himself like a man 'tracking out the confines of a lake', and discovering that it was no lake at all 'but an arm of the ocean, and that he was confronted by the immeasurable sea'.[2] Or the word might suggest 'a reservoir so deep that soundings cannot reach the bottom of it' (Mitton, NCB). Those *unsearchable riches* were not simply the gospel, not doctrine, but Christ himself (*cf*. Mt. 13:44). And the inestimable privilege of Paul's calling was to present Christ to the Gentiles

---

[1] There is a double comparative (*meizoteran*) in 3 Jn. 4, and other similar double forms were used by Greek poets and later prose writers.

[2] *The Best of John Henry Jowett*, edited by G. Kennedy (London, 1948). p. 1.

who had not heard of him before, nor been included in his kingdom (*cf.* Acts 9:15; 22:21; 26:17–18; Rom. 11:13; 15:16–21; Gal. 2:7–9).

9. In the first place the task of the apostle was simply to make known the unsearchable riches of Christ to those who had not heard of them before. But as people came to faith in him, the preacher's work was to go on to share the knowledge of the wonderful purpose of God. So Paul describes his task as 'bringing to light' (NEB) this great truth. The MSS here vary between including and excluding the word *pantas*, translated *all men* in RSV; and accordingly we have a meaning of the verb *phōtisai* that requires or does not require a personal object. The slightly more likely alternative is that *all men* should be omitted, and the verb taken (as in 1 Cor. 4:5 and 2 Tim 1:10) to mean 'showing forth' or 'bringing to light' (NEB) God's 'purpose'. The word is in fact 'the natural word to use for the public disclosure of what had been kept secret' (Robinson).

There are two further textual difficulties in this verse. The AV reading 'fellowship' translates *koinōnia*, which we now know to be the reading of only a few, less important MSS, and the weight of evidence supports *oikonomia* as the original reading. In other words, we have again the term that was used in 3:2 (as in 1:10), and RSV seems rightly to give the meaning here as God's *plan* (NEB 'purpose'). Paul is thus expressing again the fact that his work is to show and teach the great purpose of God in Christ. It is a *mystery* (as he has said in vv. 4–5) not at all fully communicated before, but by no means as afterthought in the mind of God. God is spoken of here as the one *who created all things*, in order to imply that this was his purpose from the beginning of the creation, though in his wisdom he chose to reveal it to humanity in stages. Then at the end of the verse we have a further textual variant. The words 'by Jesus Christ' of earlier versions are not in the best MSS, and probably they were added as a comment, true in itself, but such as distracts the mind from the main point here, which is not that Christ was agent in creation, but that this purpose of God reaches back into the past as far as does his creative work.

10. What was hinted at in 2:7 is now expressed specifically. This great purpose of God for the church reaches out beyond the present time. It has to be declared now to all people, but the hosts of heaven also, who know the glory of God's creation, are *through the church* to be enlightened concerning his work for human salvation. Spiritual beings, *the principalities and powers in the heavenly places*, as we have seen on 1:21, were given a prominent place in the early Gnostic systems that were being developed at this time. Paul, in accepting the existence of such beings, not only insists that all were made by Christ and are subject to him, but also shows that, in one way at least, human beings in the blood-bought church of God have a superior position to them all. They know and are to declare to these spiritual powers (*cf.* 1 Pet. 1:12) the redeeming purpose and work of the Almighty, the aspects of *the manifold wisdom of God* that otherwise they cannot know. Here, as in verse 8, a descriptive adjective is used that is pregnant with meaning. It is *polypoikilos* (the simple form *poikilos* is used in 1 Pet. 4:10), a word that means 'variegated', and that was used in classical Greek writers with reference to cloth or flowers, and so here it suggests 'the intricate beauty of an embroidered pattern' (Robinson) or the endless variety of colours in flowers. Such, the apostle says, is the *wisdom of God* that the church declares.

11. The connection of this verse with what has gone before is probably not so much that the declaration to the angels is of the eternal purpose, but that the wisdom of God is concerned with his *eternal purpose . . . in Christ Jesus our Lord*. We are back again to this great, central theme of the letter. Behind all the events of this world's history there is an *eternal purpose* being worked out. God's is no *ad hoc* plan, but one conceived from eternity and eternal in its scope. Christ is the agent of this purpose. The verb here would be literally rendered as the purpose which God 'made' or 'did'. RSV renders it as that which God *realised* – NEB 'achieved', NIV 'accomplished'. It seems more likely that it is the purpose 'which he purposed', as AV takes it, though the Greek is not quite the usual form of expression for this. The difference in meaning is not great, as this letter shows that both the beginning and the fruition of the purpose is in him, and the emphasis on his work itself is borne out by the fullness of his name in this context, which we might translate, 'the Christ, even Jesus our Lord'. Each name, that which speaks of the preparation for his coming, that which refers to his incarnate life, and that which shows his position in the whole universe, adds to our understanding of his work.

12. Now from the exalted, cosmic view, the apostle turns to the most practical significance that it has for the everyday life of the Christian. To this mighty God, whose purpose embraces heaven and earth, time and eternity, *we, in* Christ, *have boldness and confidence of access.* The word *boldness (parrēsia)* is basically 'freedom of speech'. It is often used of boldness before other people, as in 6:20, Acts 4:31 and Philippians 1:20, the absence of fear or shame. It is used of a similar absence of fear or shame in approaching God. Hebrews 4:16 and 10:19 are the clearest examples and explanations of this, which is the meaning here. Linked with this word is that which has been used already in 2:18, here translated *access;* and in the light of the following phrases it is clear that it is again the intransitive use of the word that is right (*access*, rather than 'introduction'). *Confidence of access* expresses a thought very similar to that of boldness, but it is more personal. *Faith in him* is the means of access (*cf.* Rom. 5:1–2). The forgiveness of sins that makes access possible is the gift of God's grace received by faith (Eph. 2:8–9), faith which regularly in the Pauline letters means no mere intellectual belief, but personal knowledge of and commitment to Christ.

13. Because of that freedom of approach to the eternal Lord himself, and because of the greatness of his purpose, within the scope and glory of which every Christian has been brought, Paul urges that there should be no faint-heartedness in the face of his tribulations. The difference between translations here indicates an ambiguity in the Greek which can be taken in any one of three different ways. As no subject of the second verb is expressed, it could be 'I ask that I may not lose heart . . .' (see RV mg.), but in the context this is the least likely. It could be a prayer, as RV can be understood, 'I ask that ye faint not', but this verb *aitoumai* is not normally understood as meaning 'pray' unless the name of God is mentioned as the one to whom the request is made. It is more likely, as RSV (like other translations) renders it, that we have an entreaty addressed to the readers, *I ask you not to lose heart over what I am suffering for you.* Paul was aware of the fact that they were tempted to lose heart because he, the apostle and champion of the Gentiles, was in prison. (See on 6:21–22.) This they must not do, but rather realize that his sufferings were their gain and *glory.* It was true that he was suffering imprisonment *for* them, because he had given his life to preach the gospel to the Gentiles, and because he had stood for the equality of Gentiles with Jews in the one people of God (see on 3:1). But in his willingness to do this, and in the grace of Christ given to him in imprisonment, they could glory. Their apostle was continuing to live out and show forth the sufferings of Christ (Col. 1:24), and because this was all in the loving wisdom and purpose of God, they could be sure that Christ was being magnified by Paul's weakness and confinement even more than he would be by a continuous successful mission. (*Cf.* 2 Cor. 4:7–12; 12:9–12; Phil. 1:12–14.)

D. RENEWED PRAYER (3:14–21)

14. Now Paul takes up again the words with which he began in 3:1, *For this reason,* and this time he utters his prayer. It has an added force now in the light of what he has just said. Not only is he led to prayer by the thought of the greatness of the grace of Christ raising to life those who were dead in sin, and by the realization of the unity into which Jew and Gentile have been brought in the one household, but also by the contemplation of the whole wonderful purpose of God which he has been led now to express more deeply and more personally. In the light of these things and, we have to add, the temptation of his readers to lose heart, he prays now as he does. It is a prayer like that of 1:15–23, but it has an even greater intensity, as is implied in the words *I bow my knees before the Father.* Among the Jews it was usual to stand to pray (see Mt. 6:5 and Lk. 18:11, 13). Kneeling for prayer, though it has become a regular Christian attitude, was formerly an expression of deep emotion or earnestness, and on that basis we must understand Paul's words here. Solomon knelt at the dedication of the temple (1 Ki. 8:54); Stephen at the time of his martyrdom (Acts 7:60); Peter at the death-bed of Dorcas (Acts 9:40); Paul at the time of his farewells on his last journey to Jerusalem (Acts 20:36; 21:5); our Lord himself in his agony in Gethsemane (Lk. 22:41).

15. The words 'of our Lord Jesus Christ' at the end of verse 14 in the AV were not in the oldest MSS and so are omitted in recent translations, but as is so often the case, the name of the one to whom Paul prays is qualified to bring out the depth of the meaning and significance of his prayer (*cf.* 1:17). God is not only Father, but he is also the one *from whom* alone all the fatherhood that there is derives its meaning and inspiration. This verse has been variously translated. The Greek words *pasa patria* cannot be taken as 'the whole family (AV) – the article would be required for this. The meaning therefore is not simply that all in heaven and earth have him as Father. *Every family* (RSV and also NEB) is closer. The word cannot quite be translated 'fatherhood' (RV mg.). It means strictly 'lineage' or 'pedigree' (on the father's side) or more often a 'tribe' or even 'nation', but by the context and the derivation of the word ('father' is *pater* in the Gk.), the idea of fatherhood is there. In effect the apostle is saying, think of any 'father-headed group' (Allan) *in heaven and on earth.* Each one *is named* from him. From him it derives its existence and its concept and experience of fatherhood. As Severian (quoted by Robinson) puts it, 'The name of father did not go up from us, but from above it came to us.' To such a Father, Father of all, the one in whom alone fatherhood is seen in perfection, men and women come when they come to pray.

This qualification, like that of 1:17, gives strength to prayer. With it we may compare the Lord's specific comparison between human fatherhood and the divine fatherhood in Matthew 7:11 in the matter of giving 'good things to those who ask'. We may note also the use that the apostle makes of human relationships to teach divine truth. Feminist theologians bring the challenging question whether it is right to think and speak of God as Father and not equally as Mother of us all.[1] Clearly there is no sex in God who is creator of both male and female. It is equally clear that feminine metaphors are used of God (Is. 42:14; 66:13) as also of our Lord Jesus Christ (*e.g.* Mt. 23:37). It is also true, however, without wrongly stereotyping roles, that there are in general terms distinctives of the father and the mother relationships in the family. Without denying relevance of female/mother imagery that can be related to God, we may still value highly the significance of calling God 'Father'. From the best of human fatherly relationships we can think of God as the perfect Father. From God's relationship to his family we can better understand the ideal for human fatherhood. As almighty, all-loving, all-wise Father, God initiates, provides, protects, disciplines. Our knowledge of God is helped by the suggestion that all that we know of human fatherhood at its best is true, but to an infinitely higher degree, of God in his relation to us. At the same time the concept of human fatherhood is infinitely ennobled by the comparison. Exactly the same is true of the apostle's treatment of the husband-wife relationship in 5:22–23.

16. The qualification of the name 'Father' has been added to strengthen faith for prayer. The reminder of his resources now has the same purpose. Yet again this letter speaks of *the riches* of God (see on 1:7), and the preposition is significant. Paul does not pray merely that God will give 'out of the treasures of his glory' (NEB), but *according to* them (*cf.* Phil. 4:19). He gives without limit because he himself is infinitely greater than the measure of human minds; and the riches that he gives are of his very nature (see on *glory* in 1:6).

The first gift for which prayer is made here is strength. So it was in 1:19, and, as there, this power of God is not expressed by just a single word (*cf.* also 6:10 and Col. 1:11). That they may be *strengthened with might*, the apostle prays. The verb *krataiōthēnai*

---

[1]Some feminist theologians go much further than this and argue for a feminine principle in the Deity or the value of goddess religions, and even witchcraft, in the interpretation or modification of Christian understanding. *E.g.*, see R. R. Ruether, *Sexism and God-talk* (London, 1983) and *Women/Church* (San Francisco, 1985), and D. L. Carmody, *Feminism and Christianity* (Nashville, 1982); and for a significant critique of such views D. G. Bloesch, *The Battle for the Trinity* (Ann Arbor, 1985).

speaks of being made strong or capable. A person can be made strong in love, or knowledge, or some other quality; at this point the prayer is that Paul's readers may be equipped with the power (*dynamis*) that makes them able to stand firm in Christ, and to live and work for him (*cf.* 1 Cor. 16:13; Phil. 4:13). This prayer, however, speaks further of the means and the sphere of operation of this power. It is the constant assumption, or specific emphasis, of the teaching of the New Testament, that strength for the Christian life comes by the personal indwelling of the Holy Spirit. The Holy Spirit comes into the 'inner being' (NEB). The expression is used which in 2 Corinthians 4:16 speaks of the contrast with all that is external, as Paul says 'Though our outer nature is wasting away, our inner nature is being renewed every day'. It may include, or at least it affects, all that the New Testament means when it speaks of heart, mind, will and spirit. It is the deep seat of the personality, where the *Spirit* seeks to have his dwelling and so transform the whole life of a human being.

17–18. Another way of expressing the work that it is God's purpose to do in the lives of men and women, and which therefore can be an object of prayer on behalf of others, is *that Christ may dwell in* their *hearts*. The indwelling of Christ in the heart, and the strengthening by the Spirit coming into the inner being, are not two different experiences. Paul is not always precise in distinguishing the work of Christ and of the Spirit in human lives, as Romans 8:9–10 well shows (*cf.* Jn. 14:16–18). If he were using strict theological terminology he might speak simply of the Spirit in such a context. But such is the unity of the Christ preached to them and the Spirit who indwells, that sometimes he prefers to speak as he does in this verse. The verb he uses (*katoikein*) is also significant, for it is in contrast to one that speaks of a transitory dwelling in a place (*paroikein*, from which we have the noun used in 2:19). The thought is precisely that of the hymn 'Come not to sojourn, but abide with me'.[1] Then once again *faith* is described as the human requirement, as the attitude that receives him. The Christ waits only for this

---

[1] From *Abide with me*, by Henry Francis Lyte.

willingness and desire that he should come in with all the fullness of blessing that his presence conveys (*cf.* Rev. 3:20).

His presence means not only strength, but wisdom, inspiration, and above all love; and it is to love that the prayer now turns, and love continues as its theme to the end. Grammatically the second half of verse 17 is connected with verse 18. It is possible to take the words *in love* with the first half of the verse (as in NEB). They stand before the participles, and it is true that several times in this letter the words may bring a clause to an emphatic close (1:4; 4:2, 16). Yet the phrase would seem in this case rather to overload the preceding clause, and appears to be needed with the participles. So it seems better to understand the prayer as for the indwelling of Christ by faith, and then for such a firm establishing of their lives *in love*, that they may go on to a deep understanding of God. It is thus preferable to take the whole of the participial phrase as within the clause of verse 18 (as does RSV; so also AV and RV). There is no difficulty in the mixing of the metaphors of these two participles (*cf.* Col. 2:17 and the similar combination in 1 Cor. 3:9). Both are often used by the apostle. The roots of Christian character are to go down deeply and its foundation is to be firmly laid, and love is to be the means of both.

Paul was aware of a danger, especially in the churches of the Greek world, of a faith that depended simply on intellectual knowledge (*cf.* 1 Cor. 1:22; Col. 2:18, 23; 1 Tim. 1:4; 6:4). This was the supreme weakness of Gnosticism. He is not so much arguing, however, against an approach to faith in Christ which is barren because it is merely intellectual. Rather he shows again and again that his own line of approach is totally different. He realized that 'true knowledge', the knowledge of God, 'is unattainable without love' (Scott). If there is no love, the Spirit of Christ is not present, and there can be no understanding. John 7:17 and 15:9–17 express this same fact by showing that understanding comes where there is obedience, which is the fruit of love. The impossibility of holding the faith of Christ without love is one of the great themes of 1 John. In fact these verses give two reasons why understanding proceeds of necessity from love.

In the first place, the truth is not apprehended by an

individual in isolation but *with all the saints;* and secondly the content of the knowledge and wisdom of God is love. Chapter 4:7–16 will indicate that the individual members of Christ's body can grow in understanding and in strength only as each possesses and uses for the benefit of all the varying gifts of the Spirit, gifts that make them able to work as apostles, prophets, evangelists, pastors and teachers, 'for building up the body' (4:12). It is also true that people are limited in the very understanding of the purpose of God until they see it working out, and they themselves are parts of its outworking in the 'fellowship of the saints'. The word translated *may have power* (Gk. *exischysēte*) and also the verb *comprehend* (*katalabesthai*), meaning 'an earnest grasping', suggest the difficulty of the task envisaged, simply because it is no mere intellectual feat, but a matter of practical experience, a living together in love which is inevitably costly. We are not intended to give detailed meanings to *the breadth and length and height and depth;* rather we are to feel with heart and mind and intuition the 'many dimensions' of love, and work to weave that love into all the fabric of life. Sampley (*PC*) links the thought here with that of the new temple (*cf.* 2:20–22) and thus the prayer is that believers may know 'the parameters of their new dwelling'. Or, it may be right to say with Haupt that the dimensions are of 'the redemptive plan of God in all its fulness and depth',[1] but then in that plan one comes to understand the love which there finds its expression.

19. However we interpret the dimensions of verse 17, the definite goal to which the Christian life must move, and for which therefore the apostle prays, is for his readers *to know the love of Christ*, to know how he loved and loves, and to experience his love in loving him and loving others for his sake. Yet even here Paul cannot escape the paradox. In the Greek between the verb and its object there is this qualification that apparently contradicts the verb – the love *surpasses knowledge* (*cf.* Phil. 4:7). The love of Christ is infinitely greater than anyone can fully know or imagine, and it is also much more than any object of knowledge; it is superior to knowledge (1 Cor. 8:1), even to

[1]E. Haupt, *Der Brief an die Epheser* (*Kritisch-exegetische Kommentar über das Neue Testament;* Göttingen, 1902).

spiritual knowledge (1 Cor. 13:2). It must find expression in experience, in sorrows and joys, trials and sufferings, in ways too deep for the human mind to fathom, or for human language to express.

The climax of the apostle's prayer for his fellow-Christians is that they *may be filled with all the fullness of God*. He thus prays ultimately that they may receive not any attribute of God, or any gift of his, not love, not knowledge, not strength, alone or in combination – but no less than the very highest he can pray for, the full indwelling of God. This 'defies even the beginnings of our understanding' (Stott), but we should not miss the point of what the apostle is striving to express. Of course the eternal God can never be limited to the capacity of any one, or all, of his sinful creatures; at the same time Paul does not want to pray for anything less than that God's people may be filled to (*eis*) the very fullest of himself that he seeks to bring into their lives (see on 1:23). For his own life, and for those to whom he ministers, Paul wants no less than the Spirit's full indwelling (5:18). Of his fullness, and not just of a part of his nature, all may receive (Jn. 1:16); and the goal for the individual and for the body must be nothing short of 'the measure of the stature of the fullness of Christ' (4:13).

20. Robinson well says, 'No prayer that has ever been framed has uttered a bolder request.' Yet 'unabashed by the greatness of his petition, he triumphantly invokes a power which can do far more than he asks, far more than even his lofty imagination conceives.' Often with Paul intercession takes up from praise, and here it also leads to praise because of the thought of the greatness that is the Lord's and the magnitude of the gifts that he knows he has been able to ask of him in faith. He *is able to do far more abundantly than all that we ask or think*. Other New Testament doxologies speak thus of his infinite ability (*e.g.* Rom. 16:25 and Jude 24). There is no limit to his *power*; only human words and thoughts about it are limited. This *power*, moreover, Paul will repeat, is the power 'according to' which (NIV and see on v. 16) God acts, and that not as an external force, but as that which is *at work within us*. It is present in human lives when Christ is indwelling (v. 17), and when the Holy Spirit is operative in the inner being (v. 16), energizing them there (*energoumai* – see on 1:19).

21. In the manner of most doxologies Paul says that to God *glory* is due through all eternity – *to all generations, for ever and ever.* If we are to analyse such an expression, its implication is that his praise is to go on *to all generations* to the consummation of time in eternity. The distinctive feature of this doxology lies in the two ways in which that *glory* is said to be shown and the praise declared. Firstly, it is *in the church.* The church is the sphere of the outworking of God's purpose on earth, and even in heaven it will have the task of proclaiming the manifold wisdom of God (3:10). It is never to take glory to itself (*cf.* Ps. 115:1); its goal is to give praise and glory to God (1:6, 12, 14). Then secondly, it is *in Christ Jesus* himself, for it is God's purpose 'in Christ' – Christ the beginning, Christ the saviour, Christ the source of unity – that has been the apostle's theme in these chapters. This is the goal of Paul's vision that inspires all his work. 'God is all in all. At this furthest horizon of thought, Christ and His own are seen together rendering to God unceasing glory' (Findlay). They are coupled in the infinitely wonderful purpose of God – perhaps already there is a hint of the imagery of chapter 5 and of Revelation 21 – bride and bridegroom, redeemed and redeemer. The glory of God is most gloriously seen in the grace of his uniting his sinful creatures to his eternal, sinless Son.

III. UNITY IN THE BODY OF CHRIST (4:1–16)

A. MAINTAINING THE UNITY (4:1–6)

1. As is often the case in Paul's letters, the doxology marks the end of a section. The doxology at the end of chapter 3 marks the close of the part of the letter that is predominantly doctrinal. Chapters 4 – 6 are to show in practical detail how glory is to be rendered to God now in the church (3:21). The apostle begins here as he did in chapter 3, by referring to himself as *a prisoner* (see on 3:1), but here 'the prisoner in the Lord' (RV) is the most precise translation of what is written. The chains of his imprisonment limited his bodily movement, but his life was most truly controlled by the fact that it was 'in the Lord'. The fact that his life in and for Christ had led to imprisonment did not mean that he requested the sympathy of his readers, but it added intensity to his appeal, as now he wished to speak to them concerning the whole manner of their life. He has set before them the great purpose of God in Christ for his church. He has prayed that they may know the wonder of his plan, his love, his power, and every spiritual blessing that he offers. But now in these remaining chapters he is going to write about the quality and kind of life that is demanded of them individually and in the fellowship of Christ's church.

It is no mere teaching of the Christian ethic that the apostle seeks to give. He whose greatest concern in life has become to 'present every man mature in Christ' (Col. 1:28; *cf.* Acts 20:27, 31) makes earnest entreaty. The word *parakalō* can mean 'exhort', but obviously in this context has its stronger meaning, *beg* (*cf.* 2 Cor. 5:20). The link with what precedes is given by the word *therefore* as in Romans 12:1, indicating that Christian conduct follows from Christian doctrine, that the duty of Christians derives directly from the unspeakable debt of gratitude that they owe for all that they have received in Christ. In the most general terms, that duty is that they should *lead a life worthy of* their *calling*. We are back to three great Pauline words (*cf.* 1 Thes. 2:12). Step by step they are to walk (see on 2:2) in a direction that corresponds to their call (1:18). That call to know the grace of God in Christ, to be the children of God, and to serve him as his 'dedicated ones' and messengers of his gospel, should transform every part of life. It involves the obligation to live in a manner that is in accordance with the name of him whose they are and whom they serve (Phil. 1:29), pleasing him in all things (Col. 1:10). 'Those who have been chosen by God to sit with Christ in the heavenly places must remember that the honour of Christ is involved in their daily lives.' So Bruce (*EE*) comments, adding that this first far-reaching instruction is 'a principle to guide in every situation'.

2. Four particular aspects of such a life are now named, and they are more than personal qualities. For the life worthy of the calling of God is a life in the fellowship of the people of God; and if this is to be maintained these four virtues are vital. The first, emphasized by the characteristic *all* (*cf.* 1:8; 4:19, 31; 5:3, 9; 6:18), is *lowliness*. Very significantly, the Greek noun *tapeinophrosynē* does not seem to have been used before New Testament times, and the corresponding adjective *tapeinos* nearly always had a bad meaning, and was associated with words having the sense of slavish, mean, ignoble. Lessons of humility had been taught in the Old Testament, and such a passage as Isaiah 66:2 in the Septuagint is a notable exception to the general pre-Christian use of *tapeinos*, but to the Greeks humility was not a virtue. To them, as indeed to most non-Christian people in any genera-tion, the concept of 'the fulness of life ... left no room for humility' (Robinson). In Christ *lowliness* became a virtue. His life and death were service and sacrifice without thought of reputa-tion (Phil. 2:6–7). Because the Christian is called to follow in his steps, humility has an irreplaceable part in the Christian charac-ter (*cf.* Acts 20:19), and also for the reason that he has been brought to see the greatness and glory and holiness of God, so that he cannot but be overwhelmed by the realization of his own weakness and sinfulness.

The second word, *meekness* (*prautēs*), was used in classical Greek in the good sense of mildness or gentleness of character. The adjective (*praos*), especially, found an important use in describing an animal completely disciplined and controlled. *Meekness* in the New Testament is used of a person's attitude to the word of God (Jas. 1:21), but more often of one's attitude to other people (1 Cor. 4:21; 2 Tim. 2:25; Tit. 3:2). It is closely connected with the spirit of submissiveness which becomes the keynote of this letter when, in 5:21, the apostle turns to speak of human relationships. Moses is aptly described in Numbers 12:3 as 'very meek'. For, as Mitton (*NCB*) puts it, meekness 'is the spirit of one who is so absorbed in seeking some worthy goal for the common good that he refuses to be deflected from it by slights, injuries or insults directed at himself personally, or indeed by personal considerations of any kind'.

Thirdly, there is *patience* (*makrothymia*), a word sometimes used of steadfast endurance of suffering or misfortune (as in Jas. 5:10) but more often, as is the case here, of slowness in avenging wrong or retaliating when hurt by another. It is used of God's patience with humanity (Rom. 2:4; 9:22; 1 Tim. 1:16; 1 Pet. 3:20; 2 Pet. 3:15), and the corresponding and consequent quality that the Christian should show towards others (1 Cor. 13:4; Gal. 5:22; Col. 3:12; 2 Tim. 4:2).

Forbearance, the fourth requirement, is also a divine quality (Rom. 2:4). It is the practical outworking of longsuffering. 'It involves bearing with one another's weaknesses, not ceasing to love one's neighbours or friends because of those faults in them which perhaps offend or displease us' (Abbott). It is 'that mutual tolerance without which no group of human beings can live together in peace' (Stott). Such forbearance, and indeed all these four qualities, are possible only *in love*. For love is the basic attitude of seeking the highest good of others, and it will therefore lead to all these qualities, and include them all (see vv. 15–16 and on 1:4). Paul has prayed that his readers may be 'rooted and grounded in love' (3:17), and now he exhorts them to do their part, and to go on to possess all these virtues *in love*.

3. All that now follows in the rest of the letter may be considered as an expansion of the appeal that has just been made. But its first particular application is to the unity of Christians. Some have taken *the unity of the Spirit* here to mean the spiritual unity of the church in the sense that human spirits are linked together wherever men and women are found sharing the things that they have 'in Christ'. We have noted already (on 1:17) that it is sometimes difficult to tell exactly how we should translate and interpret this word 'spirit'. Here, however, it is almost certain that the apostle views the unity as the gift of God. It was made possible by the cross of Christ (2:14ff.), and is made effective by the working *of the Spirit* of God. Human beings cannot themselves create it; it is given to them, but their responsibility is to keep it, to guard it in the face of many attempts from within and without the church to take it away. Christians are to be *eager to maintain the unity*. The Greek participle *spoudazontes* conveys the idea of zealous effort and care (*cf.* 1 Thes. 2:17; 2 Tim. 2:15; 2 Pet. 1:10, 15; 3:14).

But, as with his practical bent the apostle has in the previous verse added forbearance to 'patience', so here to the abstract 'oneness' (a word which in fact he hardly ever uses) he adds the means to such unity, which is maintained by keeping *the bond of peace*. If by love (which the parallel passage in Col. 3:14 [AV] calls 'the bond of perfectness') people can live in the peace that Christ has brought them, then unity will be kept indeed.

4. The apostle is aware of the endless variety of temperaments amongst his readers and the diverse racial and social backgrounds from which they have come into the Christian church; but he would have them even more aware of the spiritual realities that now unite them and that should completely transcend differences of background. Already, in 1:13–14, he has spoken of the spiritual blessings that are now shared between Jews and Gentiles, and in 2:11–22 of the barriers between them that have been broken down in Christ. All, he says, now have equal shares in the privileges of grace (3:6). Here, as in a credal summary, perhaps a fragment of an early Christian hymn (see on 5:19), he names what they have in common, a unity by the Spirit in the church, a unity in Christ acknowledged and confessed as Lord, a unity ultimately in God the Father and source of all. As Caird puts it, 'The corporate unity of the church is not a desirable end, but a datum to which the behaviour of its members must conform.'

They are brought to be *one body*. To be 'in Christ' means to be in his body (see on 1:1), members one of another as truly and intimately as are the organs of the human body. The unity is indeed a spiritual unity, and therefore transcends and surpasses any association or society with its basis in the things of this world. Yet we must beware of thinking of it simply as spiritual and unseen. To say 'one body' is more than to say that people are of 'one spirit'. The sense of spiritual kinship did not satisfy Paul. The apostle who was so concerned with the practical unity of Jews and Gentiles in the church, and with the working together of all Christians, would surely have abhorred many of the divisions that we accept. Where differences in essential doctrine and contradictions in ethical teaching make such divisions, he would strive to know and uphold the way of Christ in each detail. Where differences are caused merely by superficial things or by the selfish individualism of members, he would toil and fight for the breaking down of barriers and the working out of genuine fellowship. It was right and necessary for the Reformers to uphold the doctrine of the 'invisible Church' as against a view that membership of an outward organization meant *ipso facto* membership of Christ; but at the same time the New Testament shows that in the sight of God there is *one body* of Christ, and in loyalty to him Christians are impelled to strive to 'let the relations of practical Christian life and work correspond to that fact, to the utmost possible' (Moule, *CB*).

There is also *one Spirit*, and the RSV is surely right in taking it as the Holy Spirit. The following verses refer to the Father and the Son,[1] and we have a close parallel to 2:18 which has spoken of our 'access in one Spirit to the Father' (*cf.* 1 Cor. 12:13). All who are members of the one body are that by virtue of the *one Spirit* of God dwelling in them (Rom. 8:9). This fact prevents any view of the church as a mere organization; for the presence of the Spirit constitutes the church, and is the basis of its unity. Then, all who have the Spirit have a common *hope*. From a vast variety of backgrounds they have come, but their goal is now the same. The Spirit is 'the guarantee' (1:14) and the pledge that in the end all will stand together in the presence of the Lord and be restored fully to his likeness and possess his inheritance. For those who share the glory of that hope (1:18; Rom. 5:2; Col. 1:27), and are concerned to give witness of it to the world, it is folly not to strive now to keep a unity in peace and love.

5. There is also *one Lord*, even Jesus Christ. This, as 1 Corinthians 12:3 shows us, was the basic, primitive Christian creed (*cf.* 1 Cor. 8:6; Phil. 2:11). It expresses more, however, than a belief that is shared; it speaks of a common allegiance to *one* transcendent *Lord* and where this is more than mere lip-service (*cf.* Mt. 7:21) it should bind people together more than anything else. Where there is 'the same Lord' (Rom. 10:12), Jews and Gentiles, black and white, rich and poor, great and small, are yoked together. Neither personal ambition, nor party spirit, nor

---

[1]Verses 4–6 here, like 1 Corinthians 12:4–6, are verses in which the doctrine of the Trinity is implicit. Though the word Trinity is never used, in such passages the naming of Father, Son and Holy Spirit and their divine functions makes the doctrine inescapable. *Cf.* Mt. 28:19; 2 Cor. 13:14.

disputes about non-essentials will be allowed to break such unity, if Christ is served and honoured as Lord.

It is possible that the *one faith* means the same attitude of trust that binds us all to the Lord, the same way of access to him and means of life in him. Or it may be that here, and then in verse 13, it means the same vital truths concerning him and his work and purpose. This way of speaking of 'the faith' was indeed more common later (1 Tim. 3:9; 4:1, 6; Tit. 1:4; Jude 3), but it seems to be used in much this sense in Galatians 1:23 and also in Philippians 1:25 and Colossians 2:7.

The outward sign of this faith (whichever way we take it) and the 'visible word' expressing the work of Christ was *baptism*. Instituted by the Lord himself, it was an experience that every Christian shared. All had passed through the same initiation. All had been 'baptized into Christ' (Gal. 3:27), not into a variety of leaders, such as Paul, Peter and Apollos (1 Cor. 1:13), nor into a plurality of churches.[1] 'By one Spirit', Paul says in 1 Corinthians 12:13, 'we were all baptized into one body.' The sacrament is therefore a sacrament of unity. It is often asked why no reference was made here to the other great sacrament of the gospel, expressing as it did, even more obviously, the unity and the sharing that there should be between all Christians. Perhaps it is that an argument such as that in 1 Corinthians 10:16–17 would be needed to demonstrate this, rather than just a single word; or perhaps, as Westcott suggests, 'the Apostle is speaking of the initial conditions of Christian life', whereas 'Holy Communion belongs to the support and development of it'.

6. Ultimately the unity is in the *one God and Father of us all* (cf. 1 Cor. 8:6; 12:5–6). All are his creatures, made in his image as his children from the beginning, and through Christ brought back to his family (see on 1:5). Therefore all Christians belong together as brothers and sisters, and share the conviction that God is their Father, and *above all and through all and in all* (cf.

---

[1] It is often argued that the reference to *baptism* here in Ephesians, and a number of such references in the New Testament, is to baptism in or by the Spirit. It is more likely that there is specific reference to the water rite that was practised in the church from the beginning and had its antecedent in John's baptism, unless there is a specific reference to the Holy Spirit.

Rom. 11:36). Whether in a world with deities for each city or nation or aspect of life, as the world of Paul's day, or in a world which to all practical purposes has renounced God, such conviction about him should bind people more closely than any human tie. Christians believe that they 'live in a God-created, God-controlled, God-sustained, God-filled world' (Barclay), and even more, that God indwells them and is working out his purpose through them. Where can such depth and breadth of unity be found as in the fellowship of those who share this faith and experience? It follows inevitably that unnecessary divisions are folly, and weaken the church's witness in the world to such a glorious faith.

B. DIVERSITY IN UNITY (4:7–16)

7. The great heritage of the faith all Christians share, and having this in common they are responsible to guard the unity of the Spirit. But they may not expect their personalities, their gifts and their tasks to be all alike. In his wisdom, and to make each dependent on others, God has ordained not uniformity, but an endless variety of gifts for members of the body. As Calvin puts it, 'no member of the body of Christ is endowed with such perfection as to be able, without the assistance of others, to supply his own necessities.' *To each of us* is *given* different gifts for the benefit of all. Paul uses the word *grace* here in the sense in which we have found it used in 3:2, 7–8: the privilege of a special calling in the service of God. The word implies that there is no place for boasting; none has anything other than what he has received unmerited (*cf.* 1 Cor. 4:7). No-one has all the gifts; and also it is true that no member of the body is without some spiritual task and spiritual gift for it. *To each* – not ministers or leaders alone – such *grace* is given *according to the measure of Christ's gift*. These words suggest the Lord's portioning out, in his wisdom, different kinds of gifts to different members. Both the words *measure* and *grace* are used with the meaning they have here in Romans 12:3–8, while 1 Corinthians 12:4 has the same thought as this when it says that 'there are varieties of gifts, but the same Spirit'.

8. At this point Paul leads on to a new thought. 'The measure of Christ's gift' is that of the ascended Lord who in the days of his flesh promised such abundant bestowal when he returned to the Father's presence (Jn. 14:12–14). To express this the apostle quotes Scripture, Psalm 68:18, a passage which perhaps as early as this was associated with Pentecost in Jewish liturgy, and which could be applied to the triumph and ascension of the Lord followed by the bestowal of spiritual gifts to his church.[1] In their original setting the words of the Psalm picture the Lord returning in triumph (either to the Jerusalem sanctuary or to heaven itself), after the overthrow of Israel's enemies. He has made his enemies captive, and they follow, as it were, in his triumphal procession. As conqueror he has received gifts that he can bestow. Like many of the Psalms, this found ready application to the Christ. He has conquered his enemies, and returned to his Father's throne in triumph, now to bestow blessings on his people. In fact his former foes, whom he leads in 'triumph in Christ' (2 Cor. 2:14; AV, RV), like Paul himself, are his gifts to his church.

We must note, however, an important change in the words used. The Hebrew Psalm has words which speak of God 'receiving gifts among men'. Paul says *he gave gifts to men*. Various explanations have been offered for the difference. Some see it as an intentional, others as an unintentional, misquotation. It is significant that the Targum (the Jewish Aramaic paraphrase) on the Psalms, which may involve an interpretation going back into pre-Christian times, speaks of the giving rather than the receiving of gifts, as it has 'Thou ascendedst up to the firmament, O prophet Moses, thou tookest captives captive, thou didst teach the words of the law, thou gavest them as gifts to the children of men'. It is also possible that the words in this form were used in an early Christian hymn. In any case the Psalm could be understood to speak of the truth expressed in Acts 2:33: 'Being ... exalted at the right hand of God, and having received from the Father the promise of the Holy Spirit, he has poured out this ...'. The ascension of Christ made

---

[1] See further A. T. Lincoln, 'The use of the O.T. in Ephesians', JSNT 14 (1982), pp. 18ff., and also Kirby, pp. 97–99.

possible the outpouring of the Spirit (Jn. 7:39), and so these varied gifts of which he is about to speak in detail.

9–10. We have a further difficulty to deal with in these verses. When we read that *He ascended*, the meaning is clear. After his resurrection he was exalted in glory, a fact that has been emphasized already in 1:20–21 and 2:6. And when Paul says *far above all the heavens*, he uses language that agrees with the Jewish concept of a plurality of heavens, though he is not necessarily limiting himself to a spatial concept (see on 1:20). He means that Christ has been exalted to the highest honour and glory possible (Phil. 2:9–11); he has returned to the Father from whom he came into the world. But what is the meaning of his descent? The word 'first' in the AV in verse 9 is not found in the majority of the oldest MSS and it would seem that, with the more recent English versions, we should omit the word as a later interpretative addition to the text. It must be said also that the tense of RSV *had also descended* is not required by the Greek. *Ascended* and *descended* are in the same tense and same verbal forms in both verses 9 and 10. The descent may be that which Christ made by his Spirit after Pentecost. Against this is the association of the giving of the gifts with his ascension rather than his descent (in v. 8).

If the descent refers to the coming of the Spirit then *the lower parts of the earth* must mean just 'the earth below'. If it speaks of the incarnation there are further possibilities of meaning. Some have been led by these words to set this passage alongside 1 Peter 3:19 and 4:6, understood as referring to a descent of Christ after his crucifixion to preach the gospel to those who had died before his coming. The exact meaning of the 1 Peter passages is not certain, but whatever their meaning there seems no reason to suppose that there is this kind of reference here to his preaching to the dead. Above the highest heaven he ascended, and he had been to the deepest depths of the earth. This may thus mean simply this earth, so low in comparison with his heavenly home (*cf.* Is. 44:23); or it may denote the fact that he suffered the greatest humiliation when he endured death itself (*cf.* Phil. 2:8), and thus descended to what Scripture sometimes calls 'the depths of the earth' (*cf.* Ps. 69:15; Rom. 10:7).

There seem to be two points that the apostle is wanting to stress here. Firstly, it is Christ's will and purpose for everything to be pervaded with his presence (*cf.* 1:10). He has descended and ascended *that he might fill all things.* He is supreme over all the powers of heaven and earth (*cf.* Col. 1:16–18); there is nothing that is not subject to him, no place or order of existence where his presence may not be known and felt. Both the descent and the ascent have this purpose. In particular, as Barclay puts it, 'the ascension of Jesus meant not a Christ-deserted, but a Christ-filled world' because of the giving of his Spirit (*cf.* Jn. 16:7). Secondly, we are to realize that the ascended Lord whom the church now worships is the same as he who came down and lived among us, sharing our sorrows, trials and temptations, and therefore he feels those of his people today.

11. Now Paul goes on to speak of the specific gifts that he has given. The *gifts* are the people. All, in their particular ministries, are God's gift to the church. 'To Christ', says Calvin, 'we owe it that we have ministers of the gospel.' The church may appoint people to different work and functions, but unless they have the gifts of the Spirit, and therefore are themselves the gifts of Christ to his church, their appointment is valueless. The expression also 'serves well to remind ministers that the gifts of the Spirit are not for the enrichment of oneself but for the enrichment of the Church' (Allan).

At the later date which some would give to this letter it would seem almost impossible not to have reference to the local ministry of bishops, presbyters and deacons which had come to be of greatest importance to the church. As it is, the apostle is not thinking of the ministers of Christ in their offices but rather according to their specific spiritual gifts and their work, and not least of those who in the exercise of their functions were not limited to a particular locality. This may account for the differences between the list that we have here and the similar list in 1 Corinthians 12:28. It also seems true that, as F. F. Bruce puts it, 'those that are named' here 'exercise their ministries in such a way as to help other members of the church to exercise their own respective ministries'.

First stood the *apostles.* First in time and first in importance,

Masson puts it. The word *apostolos* is used in three different ways in the New Testament. It could mean simply a messenger, as is the case apparently in Philippians 2:25 – we can neglect that meaning here. It was used above all for the twelve, who in many parts of the New Testament are given a special and distinctive position (*cf.* 1 Cor. 15:5; Rev. 21:14). But we read of others as apostles, not only Paul himself and Barnabas (Acts 14:14), but James the Lord's brother (Gal. 1:19), Silas (1 Thes. 2:6), and Junias and Andronicus who are mentioned only in Romans 16:7. In fact there would appear to be those who can truly be called apostles (1 Cor. 15:7), who are not even known to us by name. From Paul's words in 1 Corinthians 9:1–2 it would seem that a necessary qualification of an apostle was to have seen the risen Lord, and to have been sent out by him, and thus to have come to be engaged as a foundation member (Eph. 2:20) and worker for the building up of the church.[1] If the qualification for an apostle was thus to have seen and been sent by the risen Lord, the proof of an apostle was his labours in the power of Christ, even 'with signs and wonders and mighty works' (2 Cor. 12:12). It should be noted also that, according to Acts 1:21–22 (*cf.* Acts 2:42), the apostles gave definitive witness to the facts of the ministry of Jesus and to his resurrection.

Closely associated with them in the work of building the church from its foundations, and therefore basic as gifts of Christ to the church, were the *prophets* (see on 2:20 and 3:5). It is harder for us to see their particular ministry, but they stand out clearly from the New Testament as people of inspired utterance, whose ministry of the word was of the utmost importance for the young church. On occasion they might foretell the future, as in Acts 11:28 and 21:9, 11, but like the Old Testament prophets their great work was to 'forth-tell' the word of God. This might be in bringing to light with convicting power people's sins (1 Cor. 14:24–25), or in bringing new strength to the church by the word of exhortation. The latter is illustrated most strikingly by Acts 15:32 where it is said that in Antioch 'Judas and Silas, who were themselves prophets, exhorted the

---

[1] The phrase 'apostles of the churches' (2 Cor. 8:23; Gk. and RSV and RV mgs.) may be taken in the non-technical sense as 'messengers' – the rendering given by AV, RV, RSV.

brethren with many words and strengthened them'.

The ministry of *apostles*, as we have understood the word above, ceased with the passing of the first generation of Christians. The foundational ministry of *prophets* ceased also. Their work, receiving and declaring the word of God under direct inspiration of the Spirit, was most vital before there was a canon of New Testament Scripture. There continued to be prophets, but not with quite the same ministry as those of the church in the first generation. The apostolic writings were coming to be read widely and accepted as authoritative; the written word took the place of the authoritative spoken word of apostles and prophets making the essential nature of the gospel plain. At the same time the local ministry came to assume much greater importance than that of itinerant ministers, and there was the added problem that there were many false teachers and self-styled 'prophets' who went from place to place to peddle their wares.

Next come the *evangelists*. Only two other references to these in the New Testament can guide us as to their function and work. In Acts 21:8 Philip, whose four daughters were prophets, is called an evangelist, and in 2 Timothy 4:5 Timothy is told to 'do the work of an evangelist'. We may assume that theirs was an itinerant work of preaching under the apostles, and it may be fair to call them 'the rank and file missionaries of the church' (Barclay).

Then, linked together (by the same article in the Gk.) are the *pastors and teachers*. It is possible that this phrase describes the ministers of the local church, whereas the first three categories are regarded as belonging to the universal church. More likely, the dominant thought is still of spiritual functions and gifts. Apostles and evangelists had a special task in planting the church in every place, prophets for bringing a particular word from God to a situation. *Pastors and teachers* were gifted to be responsible for the day-to-day building up of the church. There is no hard and fast line to be drawn between the two. The duties of the pastor (literally 'shepherd') are to feed the flock with spiritual food and to see that they are protected from spiritual danger. Our Lord used the word in John 10:11, 14 to describe his own work, and he continues to be the chief pastor (Heb. 13:20;

127

1 Pet. 2:25; 5:4) under whom others are called to 'Tend the flock of God' (1 Pet. 5:2; *cf.* Jn. 21:15–17; Acts 20:28). Every pastor must be 'an apt teacher' (1 Tim. 3:2; *cf.* Tit. 1:9), though it is evident that some have pre-eminently the gift of teaching, and may be said to form a particular division of ministry within the church, and to be a special gift of Christ to his people (Acts 13:1; Rom. 12:7; 1 Cor. 12:28).

12. Three phrases are now used in this verse to describe the purpose of the spiritual gifts just named. As different translations indicate, the three have been connected in various ways. The AV took each of them separately. The difference of the prepositions in the Greek is against this, and at least implies that the later two are dependent on the first. It is probably correct to understand the second to depend closely on the first, and the third on the two that precede: *to* [Gk. *pros*] *equip the saints for* [Gk. *eis*] *the work of ministry, for* [Gk. *eis*] *building up the body of Christ.*

In the first place, then, the ministry of the church is given to it *to equip the saints* (RSV first edition, 1946, has *for the equipment of the saints*). The word used (*katartismos*) is not found elsewhere in the New Testament, although the corresponding verb is used of repairing something (Mt. 4:21); of God's bringing the universe in the beginning into its intended shape and order (Heb. 11:3); and of restoring to spiritual health a person who has fallen (Gal. 6:1). It may be used, however, of 'perfecting' (AV) what is lacking in the faith of Christians (*cf.* 1 Thes. 3:10; Heb. 13:21; 1 Pet. 5:10) and we may say with Robinson that the word denotes 'the bringing of the saints to a condition of fitness for the discharge of their functions in the Body, without implying restoration from a disordered state'. Their being brought to this condition is not an end in itself, but for a purpose, that they may be fitted *for the work of ministry*. As clearly as in verse 7 it is thus implied that every Christian has a *work of ministry*, a spiritual task and function in the body. The word used here (*diakonia*), or the corresponding verb, is used of menial service (Lk. 10:40; 17:8; 22:26–27; Acts 6:2), and so of the particular work of those who came to be known as 'deacons', but it is also used in the more general sense of our word 'service' (see on 3:7).

What is done for the saints, and by the saints, is *for building up the body of Christ.* The word *oikodomē* has been used in 2:21, but here it has a broader meaning. The church is increased and built up, and its members edified, as each member uses his or her particular gifts as the Lord of the church ordains, and thus gives spiritual service to fellow-members and to the head. Because of its applied meaning the use of *oikodomē* with *the body* does not necessarily involve confusion of metaphors, but because of what he wishes to say now about the growth and unity of the church, the apostle finds the metaphor of the body more adequate than any other.

13. All three phrases in verse 12 have described the process going on in the life of the church. But the apostle could never think of a process without fixing his eyes on the goal. The verb used at the beginning of the verse (*katantaō*) is used nine times in Acts for travellers arriving at their destination; NEB translates 'So shall we all at last attain . . .'. (*Cf.* Acts 26:7 and Phil. 3:11 for use similar to that here.) The end of the church's journey is described in three ways. Firstly, it is *the unity of the faith.* Where *the faith* (see on v. 5) is duly communicated, people from their different backgrounds of error and ignorance come into a growing understanding of the 'one hope' (v. 4), an increasing dependence on the 'one Lord' (v. 5), and so to a developing appreciation of the 'one body' (v. 4). The goal must be *unity* in *the faith.*

Secondly, it is emphasized, though enough has already been said to make this evident, that faith is not just the acceptance of a collection of dogmas, in the embracing of which unity will be found. It is something deeper and more personal. It is unity in *the knowledge of the Son of God* (see on 1:17). That *knowledge* which Paul sought supremely for himself (Phil. 3:10) he set also as the goal for others. We can never know any person simply with our mind; and knowledge of such a person as is envisaged here must involve the deepest possible fellowship. For this person is *the Son of God,* and here we have one of the rare places in all the Pauline letters where this title is used (*cf.* Rom. 1:4; Gal. 2:20; 1 Thes. 1:10). When Paul speaks of the relation of the Lord to his church and to the Father's purpose, he regularly uses the title 'Christ', but 'when he would describe Him as the object of that

129

faith and knowledge in which our unity will ultimately be realised' (Robinson), he speaks of him in his unique position as 'the Son of God'.

But such knowledge which is fellowship with the Son of God involves the full experience of life 'in Christ', and therefore development *to mature manhood, to the measure of the stature of the fullness of Christ*. All the different expressions here speak of maturity. The Greek word *teleios* used here (RSV *mature*) has the connotation of full development in 1 Corinthians 2:6, 14:20 and Hebrews 5:14. *Manhood* here means adulthood, as in 1 Corinthians 13:11 where it is also contrasted with *nēpios*, the word used in the next verse here for 'children'. The singular, moreover, expresses again the thought that maturity involves unity; the 'many' are to become 'one new man' (2:15). Then the word that is used for *stature*, which may connote age (Jn. 9:21, 23) or physical stature (Lk. 19:3) speaks figuratively of maturity, the measure of which is nothing less than *the fullness of Christ*. As in 1:23 some interpret it here as 'the measure of the perfect Christ', made complete by his fulfilment in his church. Others take it as that which is filled by Christ. It seems better to understand it in the way that we have taken the phrase in 1:23, as the complete possession of the gifts and grace of Christ that he seeks to impart to humanity. He has himself the very fullness of God (Col. 1:19; 2:9); he seeks that the Christian should be filled with all of his endowment that can be communicated. Whether the goal can be realized in this life or not is irrelevant. The point is that the Christian is to press forward with no lesser ambition than this. This is human life as it is intended to be, measured only by all that we can understand of the human life of Christ himself.

14. There must be *no longer* the immaturity of *children* (*nēpioi*), characterized by instability in the face of the pressures of different doctrines and standards of life. 'Maturity brings with it the capacity to emulate various forms of teaching, to accept what is true and reject what is false' (Bruce, *NICNT*). The word translated *tossed to and fro* is the verb from the noun *klydōn*, used in Luke 8:24 of the raging of the waters of Galilee, and in James 1:6 for the 'surge of the sea' (RV); in the latter case it is the waves themselves that are driven by the wind, but here the picture is probably that of a boat *tossed* in the storm *and carried about*. This second verb is translated more vividly by NEB 'whirled about'; the Greek verb *peripherō* often has the idea of such violent swinging about as makes a person dizzy. Christians were realizing already that they had to keep an even keel against *every wind of doctrine*, as the companion Letter to the Colossians well shows. The unsteady and rudderless could easily be turned from their course. For there were not only those who had been deceived and gone astray without realizing it, but there were some who were lying in wait to deceive (*cf.* 2 Tim. 3:13). Their activities are described firstly by the word *kybia*, which means literally playing with dice, and hence trickery or fraud; and secondly as *craftiness* (*panourgia*), the word used with reference to our Lord's questioners in Luke 20:23, and in 2 Corinthians 11:3 of the guile of the serpent. When people wander out of the way of the truth (the Gk. *planē*, 'error' [RV], is lit. 'wandering'), they do not hesitate to use *deceitful wiles*, cunning devices, to lead others to follow them.

15. The preachers of the truth for their part cannot and must not resort to such methods (2 Cor. 4:2); they must act in all simplicity and straightforwardness, but at the same time beware of the means that their enemies may use. They are ambassadors of the truth, and are to be found *speaking the truth* and 'dealing truly' (RV mg. – the Gk. word *aletheuō* included both). Moreover, both are to be done *in love*. What is upheld, and the manner in which it is supported, are to be in complete contrast to those spoken of in verse 14. Such deceive others to make their own gain; Christians are to hold forth the truth in order to bring spiritual benefit to others, and they are to do so with a winsomeness that only love can make possible. Then, with a metaphor which is as far as possible removed from that which describes the immature as tossed about like a little boat in a storm, it is said that they will *grow* in stability and spiritual maturity. That growth is *into Christ*, the development of the life so that it is found more and more 'in' him, 'all things' (AV) and every part of life finding their centre and object and goal in relation to him and in union with him. The preposition might also be translated 'towards' or 'unto', and thus have the thought of growth towards his perfect humanity as standard, in the way that verse 13 has expressed it.

We should not imagine that the apostle thought of growth into the head. We are wise to take the imagery of growth first, and then the thought of *Christ* as *the head*. He may be spoken of as the whole body, but also in a particular way as *the head*. This has been expressed already in 1:22 and will be again in 5:23. Growth, and indeed every activity of the members, is from him as source and under his direction. The members can be healthy and strong only as each is dependent on him. The next verse develops this point.

16. *From* Christ alone, as head, the body derives its whole capacity for growth and activity and its direction as one co-ordinated, directed entity. Colossians 2:19 is closely parallel to this verse, and should be studied with it, but there the word translated *joined . . . together* is not used. Its only other use in the New Testament is in 2:21. It derives from a word (*harmos*) used for a joint or fastening in the construction of a building, or for the shoulder-joint of the body. The second participle (*synbibazomenon*) is used in a general way of bringing things or people together, and of reconciling those who have quarrelled, and of putting together facts in an argument or a course of teaching. Both participles thus give the sense of a functional unity, that is made possible among the members by the direction of the head. But after the participles the Greek is difficult. The word translated *joint* (*haphē*) has many meanings. Basically it means a 'touch', and so can mean 'contact', 'point of contact', or 'grip', and these meanings have led commentators to a variety of interpretations. Both the context and medical usage of the word for a 'joint' of the body justify the RSV rendering, and most English translations follow this. The Greek says literally 'through every joint of the supply', which probably means that it is through every joint with which the body is equipped – 'every constituent joint' (NEB) – that growth and true functioning are possible. In other words the body depends for its growth and its work on the Lord's direction, on his provision for the whole (*cf.* vv. 11–12), and on his arrangement for the inter-relation of the members as well.

Then we are brought back to a word (Gk. *energeia*) that has become familiar in this letter (*cf.* 1:19 and 3:7), as the apostle turns from the consideration of the members and the connection between them, to the whole *working properly*. *Each part*, in its place and according to its need, must have this functioning that is made possible by the 'energizing' of God in the whole. Then, yet again, the purpose of *growth* is mentioned, and it is made clear that each member does not seek its own growth but that of 'the body' (AV) as a whole (RSV has *bodily growth*), not its own upbuilding but the upbuilding of the whole. Moreover, the context makes clear that it is not increase in size of the church that is primarily in view, by members being added to it, but spiritual increase. And this increase is above all *in love*. The little phrase comes yet again (*cf.* 1:4; 3:17; 4:2; 5:2), as love determines that each member will seek the upbuilding of all. Then without doubt, if there is a caring community living *in love* and showing the truth *in love*, the numerical increase will follow.

IV. PERSONAL STANDARDS (4:17 – 5:21)

A. NEW LIFE TO REPLACE THE OLD (4:17–24)

17–18. This chapter began with a call to Christians to walk worthily of their vocation, and continued with the demand for spiritual growth in the fellowship of the body of Christ. Now, in still more practical terms, Paul describes the way in which such a call is to be followed. There must be the complete abandonment of the old way of living, and the working out of the new in personal life, and also in human relationships. Though the old life has been renounced by the Christian minority, they are living surrounded by those who still *live* (the verb is lit. 'walk' as in 2:2) in the darkness of their godlessness. So a warning is necessary, and it is expressed in the strongest terms: *Now this I affirm and testify in the Lord*. This word translated *testify* (*martyromai*) has probably 'lost its association with the law court' (Caird) and is used (as in Acts 20:26 and Gal. 5:3) to introduce a solemn declaration. NEB translates it, 'I urge it upon you'.

Moreover it is from one who lives *in the Lord* to others whose life is so to be lived. He is writing to those who by race are Gentiles, but who, by the transforming grace of Christ, have come to be different from 'other Gentiles' (AV). In fact the reading which has the greatest support of the old MSS here omits the word 'other', to indicate that from being Gentiles before, they now in effect had become members of the Israel of God (Gal. 6:16). In spiritual rather than racial terminology the implication here is that in the past they 'were Gentiles' (1 Cor. 12:2, AV), 'alienated from the commonwealth of Israel' with all that that involved (see 2:12), but that they are so no longer.

The true nature of that old way of life is described now in a series of devastating phrases, quite closely comparable to the expressions of Romans 1:18–31. It is true that there were some noble figures in the ancient world of Greece and Rome in which Paul lived, but classical literature as it throws light on the life of the masses indicates that the apostle's description was not wide of the mark. There was a mental, spiritual and moral decadence in that society. The prevalent way of people's living was futile (*cf.* 1 Pet. 1:18) because, as the apostle says, *futility* was characteristic of *their minds*. 'In losing the living conception of a living God', pagan society had 'lost also the conception of the true object and perfection of human life; and so wandered on aimless, hopeless, reckless' (Barry). It is not implied that all that is said in this section is true of all who are not Christian, but it is not unfair to say that 'this is the direction in which every life is facing which is out of touch with God; and this is the kind of life which will be reproduced in a community in which Christian influence is not active'.[1] Without the knowledge of God, ultimately all is vanity, as there is no sense of purpose. There may be much knowledge (*cf.* Mt. 11:25; 1 Cor. 1:18–25), but there is no light of wisdom in the mind, the *understanding* is *darkened*. Then as the knowledge of God involves more than the mind (see on v. 13), and as knowledge of God means fellowship with him, so ignorance involves 'a stance' affecting the whole of a person's life, 'emotion, will and action' (Barth, *AB*). It means being *alienated from the life of God* (*cf.* 2:1). The word *alienated* may or may

[1]W. M. F. Scott, *The Hidden Mystery* (London, 1942), p. 63.

134

not convey the sense of being estranged from what was once possessed. From one standpoint it was no fault of their own if the saving and life-giving knowledge of God in Christ had not come to them. From another standpoint, they, in common with all people, had sinned against the light that they had (Rom. 1:18–23; 2:12–15). There had been a *hardness of heart* for which they could not disclaim all responsibility. The word rendered *hardness* by RSV comes from a verb that means to 'petrify' or 'cause a callus to form', and so figuratively 'to become hard' or 'insensitive'. The noun that we have here, or the corresponding verb, is used eight times in the New Testament. In Mark 3:5 and 8:17 it refers to an attitude that is certainly culpable. *Hardness* in the sense of 'stubbornness' may be a little too strong. As Robinson puts it, 'It seems not to indicate a stubborn refusal . . . and yet not an ignorance that is completely unblameworthy.'[1] The NEB translating 'their minds have grown hard as stone' gives the idea of an insensitivity to the finer things which characterizes a life that is lived without regard for God or for moral values.

19. This thought is carried further as they are described as having *become callous*, having ceased to have any appreciation of the truth of God or any feeling of shame in the face of evil. The original force of the word is to have no more pain or sorrow, and so can be applied here to indicate that 'they have deadened their conscience and do not feel its stings' (Lock; *cf.* 1 Tim. 4:2). Immorality of life has inevitably followed. They *have given themselves up*, 'abandoned themselves' (NEB), to a life that is a betrayal of their true selves. It is a life of *aselgeia*, a word that means *licentiousness* or 'wanton violence' (LS), outrageous conduct of any kind, a life without any care for personal standards or social sanctions. Shamelessly they have given themselves *to practise every kind of uncleanness*. The noun for *practise* (*ergasia*) can mean (as in Acts 16:16, 19; 19:24) business or the gains of business, and so the thought here may be that of making a trade of impurity (as RV mg. suggests). This, however, would be unfair as a description of the Gentile world in general, but at least the

---

[1] See Robinson, pp. 264ff., for a long discussion of the meaning and New Testament use of the word.

word implies that such *uncleanness* has become, as Moule puts it, an 'earnest pursuit' or 'occupation' (*CB*).

The word that follows (*pleonexia*), qualifying *uncleanness*, means essentially being *greedy*, the desire for more than is one's due, and the passion to possess it without regard for what is right or for the persons of others. It does not always have the force that the word 'covetousness' (RV mg.) has acquired in English. In the use of the word in the New Testament it is often closely linked with the sins of the flesh. This is the case in all three passages where it is used in this letter (here and in 5:3, 5), and also in Colossians 3:5 and 1 Thessalonians 4:6 (the corresponding verb). It may be best to say that the word fundamentally means 'greed' for what is not one's due; sometimes in the New Testament it is used for the desire for money (Lk. 12:15; 2 Cor. 9:5), at other times its context gives it the force that it evidently has here of the passion for sexual indulgence at others' expense. In this connection see Hebrews 13:4–5 where the thought of one kind of greed seems to lead naturally to the thought of the other.

20–21. 'But you', the apostle says to his readers, emphasizing the personal pronoun, 'can no longer walk in that way. *You did not so learn Christ!* The truth of God and of his purpose has come to dominate your minds, and this truth has ethical implications. Your lives are no longer dark, your minds no longer vain. You are no longer alienated but walking step by step in the full light of the Lord, and in fellowship with him. So you must finish with all immorality, and the passion for what is impure, and for what outrages the souls and bodies of others.'

Moreover those who have come to recognize that they are Christ's *have heard about him*, and been *taught in him*. This last phrase *in him* thus repeats the key phrase of the letter. Christ was not only the subject, but 'the sphere of the instruction' (Robinson). With gentle irony the apostle adds force to his argument here. The words *assuming that* render the same little words *ei ge* which we have had in 3:2, and as we have seen there the challenge is to 'the reader to verify the statement' (Moule, *CB*), and as a result to make sure in no way to act as if the voice of the living Christ had not been heard. The way that these two verses are expressed may imply a form of catechetical instruction given to all new Christians. The words *as the truth is in Jesus* certainly imply, as Caird puts it, 'the whole truth about the unseen Christ in whom they are to have their new being is embodied in the historical life, death and resurrection of the man Jesus'. 'The man who bore in history the name of Jesus provides the moral content' of what is Christian. 'The Sermon on the Mount and the cross for ever exclude the union of faith and immorality' (Masson).

22. The imperatives that begin verses 22, 23 and 24 in RSV are infinitives in the Greek, where the construction links verses 21 and 22–24 in such a way that we might render it, 'The truth in Jesus is that you *put off* . . . be renewed . . . put on . . .'. The metaphor that we now have to express the change of life that there is when a person comes to be 'in Christ' is a familiar Pauline and early Christian one. Indeed it is so frequent in the New Testament letters (*e.g.* Rom. 13:12; Col. 3:9; Heb. 12:1; Jas. 1:21; 1 Pet. 2:1) that it is one of those things that have led to the suggestion of the existence even in apostolic times of a basic Christian catechism containing material that was used in the instruction of catechumens as to the meaning of new life in Christ.[1] The old is to be *Put off* and the new to be 'put on' (v. 24); and if a figure taken from dress might seem to indicate a merely superficial change, we should see the point as the complete setting aside of the old 'garments', having nothing further to do with them, and replacing them by new ones. What is to be *Put off* is described as the *old nature*. As past sins are dealt with by the grace of forgiveness, and as repentance determines to abandon them completely, all that belongs to the old way of life, the way of the heathen that has been described in verses 17–19, is to be set aside decisively. (The Gk. aorist signifies a single act.) That *manner of life* was *corrupt* and corrupting. The participle may mean 'perishing' (*cf.* Rom. 8:21; 2 Cor. 4:16; Gal. 6:8) or 'rotten' and 'polluted' (*cf.* 2 Cor. 11:3). Perhaps both meanings are present here (see note on the negative of the same root in 6:24). The *lusts*, the self-centred desires that belong to that old

[1]See p. 34 and E. G. Selwyn, *The First Epistle of St. Peter* (London, 1949), pp. 393ff.

way of life, are *deceitful* in that they promise joy and gain but cannot fulfil the promise. The whole Bible, from the story of humanity's first temptation, presents the persuasion to sin as deceit (*cf.* Mt. 13:22; Rom. 7:11; Heb. 3:13). It leads to the pollution and the spoiling of what God has made and planned, and in the end causes the doer to perish in it (Jn. 3:16; 2 Thes. 2:10).

23. The 'old nature' (v. 22) is to be put off, and Christians are to *be renewed*. Greek has two adjectives for new: *kainos*, which means new in the sense of fresh and distinctive, and *neos*, which mean new in the sense of young.[1] Both have corresponding verbs that are used in the New Testament concerning life in Christ. In 2 Corinthians 4:16 and Colossians 3:10 there is that which is formed from *kainos*, which thus has the sense of the new creation of God, replacing that which is old by a new kind of life that was not known before (see on 2:15). Here we have the verb from *neos*, which thus implies 'putting off the decrepitude of the old nature' and the 'regaining' of 'undying youth' (Barry). The present tense emphasizes further that what is required, and made possible in Christ, is continuous renewal. The place of this constant renewal or rejuvenation is *the spirit of their minds*. The construction here impels us to take *pneuma* as the human spirit and not the divine Spirit, though the expression is without parallel in the New Testament. 'Because the decay was initiated by the futility of minds alienated from God, the reversal of the process must begin with the renewal of the mind' (Caird). Such renewal in the mind (Rom. 12:2) or in *the spirit of* the mind, is possible by the indwelling of the Spirit of God. Then indeed there will be a new way of thinking and in consequence a new way of life.

24. Now *kainos*, the second word for new, is used; for in the place of the old nature, characterized by selfishness and sin, and bound by evil and its consequences, there is *the new nature* which is God's creation (see on 2:10, 15; and *cf.* 2 Cor. 5:17; Gal. 6:15; Col. 3:10; Tit. 3:5). Here, moreover, the aorist verb again implies a decisive act, putting on this God-created, God-given

---

[1] For a discussion of the two adjectives see *TDNT*, 3, pp. 447ff.

life, as it has already implied the decisive putting off of the old. The two truths of this verse and the last need to be kept before the Christian. As Westcott puts it, 'Two things are required for the positive formation of the Christian character, the continuous and progressive renewal of our highest faculty, and the decisive acceptance of "the new man".' This *new nature* is *created after the likeness of God*. So RSV renders it though the word *likeness* is not present in the original. Some would prefer to take the meaning as 'according to God's will and purpose', but the parallel in Colossians 3:10 may be taken to interpret what is said here. There 'the new nature' is said to be 'renewed in knowledge after the image of its creator'. Humanity was made in God's image in the beginning (Gn. 1:27) and when that image had been marred by sin and the life in fellowship with God lost, there was in Christ a new creation, a restoration to the divine image with all that means. Above all, the image of God is shown in character *in true righteousness and holiness*. If these qualities are not seen, at least in some measure, there is no evidence that there has been God's work of re-creation at all. In Philo and Plato, as well as in the New Testament, *righteousness* is used of the fulfilment of one's duty to other people, and *holiness* of observing one's duty to God. (In Lk. 1:75; 1 Thes. 2:10 and Tit. 1:8, as here, the two words, or their cognate forms, stand together.) RSV translates by the adjective *true* what should be rendered more strictly as 'of the truth'. Probably there is a deliberate contrast between what has been said already (especially in v. 22) to be the fruit of deceit, and such *righteousness and holiness* as come into the character when the truth as it is in Jesus is embraced and followed. (*Cf.* the similar contrast in vv. 14–15.) NEB speaks of 'the new nature of God's creating, which shows itself in the just and devout life called for by the truth'.

B. TRUTH AND LOVE TO REPLACE FALSEHOOD AND BITTERNESS
(4:25 – 5:2)

25. The last section has spoken in general terms of the putting off of the old life characterized by ignorance, futility and deceit, and so impurity and lust. In its place there must be put on the new nature, that means a new way of life characterized by holiness and righteousness. In this section the apostle turns to speak quite specifically of the sins that are to be put off, and the positive qualities or types of action that must be found in the Christian's life. There is a pattern of negative prohibition, positive command and motivation in these verses. Firstly, in contrast to the word 'truth' that ends verse 24 in the Greek, there is the way in which *falsehood* must be put away. AV has 'lying', and it is probably the speaking of what is untrue that is particularly, though not solely, in mind (see on the opposite quality in v. 15). For in place of such *falsehood* the duty of *every one* to *speak the truth with his neighbour* is to be recognized. These words are a quotation of the Septuagint of Zechariah 8:16, but with a significant little change. The preposition 'to' becomes *with*, thus indicating the inter-personal relationships that are emphasized in the clause that follows.

We are members one of another. For his argument against falsehood, Paul does not simply appeal to the moral law that his readers knew well.[1] Rather he insists that Christians break the bonds of love and fellowship by which they have come to be bound when they try to deceive one another. They belong together as members of the one body (*cf.* Rom. 12:5), and so must be completely honest with one another. Chrysostom aptly says, 'If the eye sees a serpent, does it deceive the foot? if the tongue tastes what is bitter, does it deceive the stomach?' Lying is a gross hindrance to the proper functioning of the body. When members are open and perfectly truthful one with another, the body will work in harmony and therefore efficiently. Without openness and truth, there can only be disunity, disorder and trouble in human community.

26. Another mark of the old nature is plain bad temper, unjustified anger. Quoting the Old Testament again, the Septuagint of Psalm 4:4, he says, *Be angry but do not sin.* The AV rendering of the psalm, 'Stand in awe, and sin not', gives a different turn to it. The Hebrew verb *ragaz* means basically to

---

[1]For a valuable study of Pauline ethics, and of the arguments that Paul gives, especially in this letter, see Findlay, pp. 305ff. See also C. A. Anderson Scott, *Christianity according to St. Paul* (Cambridge, 1966), pp. 197ff.

'tremble', and it could be with fear or rage (BDB). Whichever was the psalmist's thought, the Septuagint is meaningful and relevant. There is anger which is righteous anger, such as we see in our Lord himself (*e.g.* Mk. 3:5; Jn. 2:13–17); but his anger never led to sin, because his emotions were kept under perfect control. Christians must be sure that their anger is that of righteous indignation, and not just an expression of personal provocation or wounded pride. It must have no sinful motives, nor be allowed to lead to sin in any way.

Moreover, the apostle, with his sure knowledge of human nature, is aware that what begins as righteous anger 'against sins' very easily becomes perverted and soured and 'is turned against our brethren' (Calvin). Therefore he adds the wise practical instruction, *do not let the sun go down on your anger*. There is a noteworthy change in the word used here. It is more strictly 'provocation' (*parorgismos*; the corresponding verb is used in 6:4), the personal resentment that righteous anger can become when harboured and brooded over in the heart. Passionate feelings against people or their actions are not to be kept long, lest they break down the love that seeks to bring good out of evil. It is possible that Paul in giving this advice was consciously following what the Pythagoreans recommended. Plutarch said that 'if betrayed into angry reviling (they) made it their rule to shake hands before sunset'. But perhaps Psalm 4:4 was still in his mind. For that verse quoted goes on, 'commune with your own hearts on your beds, and be silent', and Paul knew that such communing was impossible unless anger had been set aside before going to bed.

27. This verse is perhaps to be linked closely with what has gone before. The danger of anger is that it gives an *opportunity to the devil*. It gives him 'a half-open door' (Moule, *CB*), an opportunity of fostering the spirit of pride or hatred. Sudden instinctive indignation against injustice or wrong, good in itself, if retained and nursed (NEB) as a grievance, will let the devil lead his victim on to unkind thoughts, words and actions, and so work havoc with personal relationships. The devil is to be resisted (Jas. 4:7), and given no place whether it is the individual's spiritual life, or the welfare of the fellowship that is in danger (*cf.*

1 Pet. 5:8–9). As we have noted,[1] Paul usually employs the word 'Satan' for the evil one, and not *the devil*. This has led some, at least from the time of Erasmus and Luther, to take the word *diabolos* in the literal sense of 'slanderer', but the use of the word in 6:11 and the common non-Pauline use are against this.

28. Turning to another characteristic of the old life, at least in some of his readers, he says *Let the thief no longer steal*. There were those in the communities to which he addressed himself, as Paul makes specific in 1 Corinthians 6:10–11, who had been in the habit of making a living by pilfering (the present participle in the Gk. of v. 28 implies this rather than a thief in any other sense). There must be no more of such practices, but honest toil instead. The word for this (*kopiaō*) signifies the strenuous work that produces fatigue, a word used in 1 Timothy 4:10 and 5:17 for earnest Christian service, but used for Paul's own manual labour in 1 Corinthians 4:12. The Christian is never to be ashamed or afraid of hard work; it is the duty of all (1 Thes. 4:11; 2 Thes. 3:10–12).

Moreover, rejecting all that in any past employment has been dishonest in any shape or form, he is to do *honest work with his hands*. Thus yet again Paul turns from the negative to the positive. Instead of robbing others of the fruit of their labour, Christians are to work for their own living. More than that, they are to work to *be able to give to those in need*. The Christian motive for earning is not merely to have enough for oneself and one's own, and then perhaps for comforts and luxuries, but to have in order to give to the needy. The Christian philosophy of labour is thus lifted far above the thought of what is right or fair in the economic field; it is lifted to the place where there is no room for selfishness or the motive of personal profit at all. Giving becomes the motive for getting. We may note the place that giving to the poor had with our Lord and his disciples, in precept and practice, though their resources must have been very slender (Mt. 19:21; Lk. 14:13; Jn. 13:29). Then from the beginning the church felt a great responsibility in this direction (Acts 2:44–45; 4:32–37; 6:1–3). Paul himself laid great emphasis

[1] See p. 42.

on provision for the poor (Rom. 15:26–27; 2 Cor. 8 – 9; Gal. 2:10), and was an example, in spite of all his labours in the ministry of the word, both in working with his hands for his own support (1 Thes. 2:9; 2 Thes. 3:8–9), and also in supporting others in need (Acts 20:34–35).

29. Now the apostle turns back to consider the Christians' speech and conversation. Not only are they to shun all that is deceitful, but all 'bad language' (NEB). The adjective used in the Greek (*sapros*) basically means 'rotten', and then has a derived sense of 'worthless'. It is talk that is 'rotten' and that 'spreads rottenness' (Barry) like bad fruit, worthless and leading others to think on the worthless. To replace this there is to be what can be described plainly and simply as *such as is good* (*cf.* Phil. 4:8). RSV *for edifying, as fits the occasion*, could be literally rendered 'for edifying of the need'. The particular Greek word *chreia* in Acts 6:3 speaks of a 'matter in hand', and so here we might translate 'for the edifying of the matter in hand'; 'words suitable for the occasion', Phillips aptly turns it. The thought is that of Proverbs 15:23, 'a word in season, how good it is!' (*cf.* Ecclus. 20:6–7, 19). As with the consideration of work and wages, the Christian standard is lifted above personal expediency, even above the question of moral right or wrong. The test of a person's use of money is, 'What am I giving to those in need?' The test of conversation is not just 'Am I keeping my words true and pure?' but 'Are my words being used to *impart grace to those who hear?*' The *grace* of the Lord's own words, the love and blessing which they conveyed, is spoken of in Luke 4:22. The utterance of the Christian is to be characterized by the same *grace* (*cf.* Col. 3:16; 4:6).

30. The instructions about anger were followed by the warning against giving place to the devil (v. 26). These instructions now about the Christian's conversation are followed by the warning *do not grieve the Holy Spirit of God*. All sin – the reminder is necessary – and not least that of the tongue, is a cause of personal sorrow to God, for we are called to fellowship with him. The preference to *the . . . Spirit*, rather than to Christ or to the Father –probably derived from Isaiah 63:10 – is particularly apt in that the Spirit is the bond of the life of fellowship, and the sin of offending a brother or sister by false word or act especially grieves him. Perhaps also, as Robinson suggests, the Spirit 'specially claims to find expression in the utterances of Christians' see (5:18–19), and the 'misuse of the organ of speech is accordingly a wrong done to, and felt by, the Spirit who claims to control it'. We are so accustomed to *the Holy Spirit* as a title for the third person of the Trinity (*e.g.* Acts 1:2, 8) that we forget the significance of the adjective. It is thrown into emphasis in the Greek here, and so kept as an adjective 'holy' rather than as a title in some translations (*e.g.* AV). *The . . . Spirit of God* who indwells us now is *holy*. Furthermore, by him Christians are *sealed for the day of redemption*. The Spirit's presence now is the seal and assurance of the life and inheritance that Christians will possess fully in the end, and the very contemplation of that should lead them to purify their lives (1 Jn. 3:2–3). There may be here the thought also of the work of the Spirit as keeping the Christian inviolate under his seal for the day of redemption (Scott).

31. Once more the apostle turns back to those sins that so readily find expression in speech, in order finally to set over against them the way that has been learnt in Christ. Six things are named here decisively to *be put away*. Firstly there is *bitterness* (*pikria*), which Aristotle spoke of as 'the resentful spirit which refuses reconciliation'. In his typical way the apostle says that *all* of this (see on 4:2) must go, every trace of such sharpness of temper. Then come *wrath* (*thymos*) and *anger* (*orgē*), named together also in Romans 2:8 and Colossians 3:8 (*cf.* Rev. 16:19; 19:15), and to be distinguished as the outburst of passion (*cf.* Lk. 4:28; Acts 19:28) is from the settled feeling of anger. *Orgē* is used for the wrath of God (see 5:6), and the verb is used in verse 26 for righteous human anger. Here it is used for the anger that springs from personal animosity, the flaring up of passion and temper because of personal provocation; and the only Christian rule concerning this is total abstinence. Then follows the word *kraugē*, translated *clamour*, 'the loud self-assertion of the angry man, who will make every one hear his grievance' (Findlay). *Slander* translates the Greek *blasphēmia*, a word often used in the

Bible for speaking against God, but also common for slanderous or abusive speaking against one's fellows (*cf.* 1 Cor. 10:30; Col. 3:8; Tit. 3:2). Lastly the apostle adds *all malice*, purposing by 'an inclusive word to gather up all that has been specified and anything else of a similar kind not precisely mentioned' (Mitton, *NCB*).

32. The eradication of evil words and actions depends ultimately on the purification of the thought life. So speaking positively, the apostle says, *be kind to one another, tenderhearted . . .* The parallel Colossians 3:12 says, 'Put on then, as God's chosen ones, holy and beloved, compassion, kindness, lowliness, meekness, and patience'. Three of these Paul has spoken of in this chapter in verse 2; here he dwells on the others. Kindness, used of God in 2:7, is urged here as a fundamental Christian virtue. It is love in practical action; as Barclay puts it, it is 'the disposition of mind which thinks as much of its neighbour's affairs as it does of its own'. In adding *tenderhearted* (*eusplanchnoi*), a word used elsewhere in the New Testament only in 1 Peter 3:8, the apostle makes sure that he cannot be understood as requiring acts of kindness without a heart of sympathy and love prompting them (*cf.* 1 Cor. 13:1–2).

He knows, however, that the obstacle to kindness and compassion is often the sense of wrong done to one, or a grievance nursed; so he goes on to speak of *forgiving one another*. The word can have the wider meaning of 'dealing graciously' with one another, but this includes forgiveness, which is probably the dominant thought here. In Colossians 3:13 the addition 'if one has a complaint against another' makes this meaning quite specific. The supreme example and motive for all Christian forgiveness is God's own forgiveness. *God in Christ*, the RSV rightly translates (*cf.* 2 Cor. 5:19), *forgave you*. He has done this once and for all and completely. Therefore in love and gratitude to him men and women must forgive. The gospels indeed emphasize that God's forgiveness cannot be received by the heart which is itself unforgiving (see *e.g.* Mt. 6:12, 14–15; 18:21–35). But the word *as* (*kathōs*) means more than 'because'; there is to be a real likeness between the forgiveness of God and the Christian's forgiving. The Christian's forgiving of others is to be

145

as free and complete as that of God, who puts away a person's sins as far as the east is from the west, and holds them against him no more.[1]

5:1. In this matter of forgiving, the calling of Christians is to *be imitators of God*. The word here (Gk. *mimētai*) is used a number of times in the New Testament for the following of a human example, but only here of imitating God himself. Furthermore, the verb is more strictly 'become'. Those who by grace are made *children* of God are by constant perseverance, and imitation of the divine copy (*cf.* 1 Pet. 2:21), to become more like the heavenly Father (*cf.* Mt. 5:44–45, 48; Lk. 6:36). Given the unbelievable privilege and grace of being his *beloved*, they are to respond in showing 'self-forgetting kindness' (Moule, *CB*).

2. In fact the apostle would broaden the sphere of 'imitation of God' from simply the forgiving spirit to *love* in every other way. The constancy with which such love is to be demonstrated is indicated by yet another use of the word *walk* (see on 2:2). *Love* is to characterize the Christian's daily progress along the road of life. Indeed this verse sums up the whole section, and sets aside all the negatives with its one great positive command. There is a perfect example, even in human flesh, which has been given and can be copied. Love answering love, love motivated by love, love made possible by the initial love of Christ, is one of the great themes of the Johannine literature (see Jn. 13:34; 1 Jn. 4:10–11; *etc.*); it is equally a great theme with Paul – it is he who has given us 1 Corinthians 13.

As in 4:32, the conjunction *kathōs* indicates a standard of comparison, and particular practical outworkings of love seen in the life of Christ are to be followed in the life of the Christian. His love was expressed in giving, and that to the point of *sacrifice* (*cf.* Gal. 2:20). The implication is that the Christian's love is

[1]Here and in the next verse the MSS vary between 'us' and 'you' and it is not possible to be sure which was written in each place. 'One reason why Greek manuscripts oscillate so much between *hēmeis* ('we') and *hymeis* ('you') is that the pronunciation of these two pronouns was almost identical in the first century AD and onwards. Hence if a scribe was copying by dictation he might well put the one for the other, especially in a context like this, where either pronoun makes good sense' (Bruce, *EE*).

similarly to be expressed in giving and sacrifice. In verse 25 of this chapter the apostle applies this to the love of husbands for their wives. In 1 John 3:16 it is made to apply generally, and that verse says more specifically what is implied here, namely that his laying down his life demands the response of our laying down 'our lives for the brethren' (*cf.* Jn. 15:12–13). However, there is not a single place in Paul's writings, nor in the New Testament generally, where the death of Christ can be spoken of as only an example to be followed, without the further expression of its atoning significance. This is stated here when it is said that *for us* he died, presenting himself an *offering and sacrifice to God*. There is no point in the argument of some commentators that the reference to his offering himself is here unrelated to the human need of forgiveness. It is not directly connected with the exhortation of 4:32, but the terms of the Old Testament sacrificial ritual are used, and his death is described as being *for us*.

The two words here, *prosphora* and *thysia*, are used together in the Septuagint of Psalm 40:6 (quoted in Heb. 10:5), and the former may perhaps be taken to refer to the whole life of obedience, and the latter in particular to his sacrificial death, but New Testament usage does not permit us to stress this distinction. The leading thought here is concerning that which in the beloved Son, and so in those who in him as 'beloved children' (v. 1), pleases the Father. The Old Testament sacrifices were spoken of as a 'sweet savour' (AV), to express metaphorically their acceptibility before God (Gn. 8:21; Ex. 29:18, 25, 41; Lv. 1:9, 13, 17). To an infinitely higher degree was the sacrifice of Christ pleasing to the Father. To our eyes the cross can only present, as F. B. Meyer says, an 'awful scene of horror', but 'in love so measureless, so reckless of cost, for those who were naturally unworthy of it', there was an action that 'filled heaven with fragrance'.[1] So by implication the life that those who are in Christ live in sacrificial self-giving to God and to their fellows has a fragrance before God and in the world. The other two Pauline uses of the same expression illustrate the point. To the apostle such was the fragrance of the gifts of the Christians in

---

[1] F. B. Meyer, *Ephesians: A devotional Commentary* (London, 1953 reprint), p. 48.

147

Philippi (Phil. 4:18), and thus he thought of his own life-calling, to be an 'aroma of Christ to God' (2 Cor. 2:14–16) and to spread 'the fragrance of the knowledge of him' (*cf.* also Jn. 12:3).

C. LIGHT TO REPLACE THE DARKNESS (5:3–14)

3. In 4:17–24 Paul has spoken in general terms of putting off the old nature and putting on the new. In the last section (4:25 – 5:2) he has spoken more particularly of putting aside deceitfulness and personal animosities, and of their replacement by truth and love in word, thought and action. Now suddenly we are turned from the contemplation of the self-giving, sacrificial love of Christ, to love's perversion in adultery and sexual abuse. The apostle knew the dangers to which his readers were exposed in the life of their society, and so spoke frankly about them.[1] Fornication and sexual perversion of almost any kind might be included under the word *porneia* (translated *immorality* by RSV first edition, 1946). Mitton (*NCB*) says it involves 'any sexual indulgence outside the permanent relationship of marriage, in circumstances where the sexual appetites are used merely as a means of pleasure without any sense of responsibility or care for the partner'. Such immorality may be regarded either as *impurity*, or as *covetousness* (NEB 'ruthless greed') in the sense in which the word *pleonexia* has been used already in 4:19. The *or* supports our argument in the comment on that verse that 'greed' is being applied in these passages specially to the 'sins of the flesh' (see Col. 2:11, AV). Immorality is uncleanness or impurity because purity means the control and direction of sexual powers and impulses in accordance with the law and purpose of God. It is 'ruthless greed' because it is selfish indulgence at the expense of others. Such abuse of God-given powers and such contradiction of the loveliness of God's pattern of living should *not even be named among* them. The expression recalls the Old Testament prohibition of mentioning even the names of the gods of the heathen and of speaking of the manner

[1] Barclay, pp. 191f., 199ff., gives a picture of the life of the Graeco-Roman and Jewish world that is very relevant as a background to Paul's instructions here, and to his words on marriage in verses 22–33.

of their worship (Ex. 23:13; Dt. 12:30; Ps. 16:4). It is incongru-
ous for those who are called to be *saints* (see on 1:1) to take any
pleasure in talking about such things, by their conversation to
approve or condone, or by gossip to make light of the sins of
others, or to excite sexual passion in the unwary (see also v. 12).

4. Before he turns to the positive side the apostle uses three
more words to describe the conduct and conversation that is to
have no place in the Christian's life. Firstly there is *filthiness*
(*aischrotēs*), more general than the *aischrologia*, 'foul talk', of
Colossians 3:8. All that is shameless, all that would make a
morally sensitive person ashamed (*cf.* Rom. 6:21) must be
excluded. Then he forbids *silly talk*, the kind of talk, Plutarch
says, that comes from a drunken man, words without either
sense or profit. Also forbidden is *levity*, distinguished by Findlay from the previous word as the idle talk of the clever man is
from that of the stupid. The usage of this word *eutrapelia* in
classical Greek was not derogatory. It could mean 'versatility'
or 'witty repartee', but the context here indicates what is *not
fitting* for the Christian. Paul is not saying that the Christian
should always be solemn, but probably he was thinking of 'the
lightness of witty talk' that plays 'too often on the border-line
of impropriety' (Robinson).

With a play on words he urges the replacing of *eutrapelia* by
eucharistia – 'let the grace of wit be superseded by the truer
grace of thanksgiving', Robinson renders it. Calvin and others
have taken *eucharistia* to mean 'gracious speech' and 4:29 has
spoken of the replacement of 'corrupt speech' (RV) by conversation that gives 'grace'. The Greek noun is not known to have
been used with this wider meaning, though the corresponding
adjective was so used. At least we may take it as *thanksgiving* in
the widest sense. Paul will have more to say about the grace of
gratitude in verse 20. Here he wants to insist that *thanksgiving*
is the best use of speech. He does not prudishly forbid
speaking about sex, nor austerely debar humour, but he would
have none of the 'flippant talk' (NEB) that harms the spiritual
life. Rather he would demand that if conversation is about sex,
or possessions, or people, it should be directed by the spirit of
thanksgiving and praise (*cf.* Heb. 13:15; 1 Pet. 4:11), towards

seeing and acknowledging the loveliness and beauty of God's gifts. If this is the case, then speech will be kept pure and uplighting.

5-6. The apostle has solemn words to say about the consequences of such sins as those he has just enumerated in people's lives. They, in common with all unrepented sins, exclude men and women from God's kingdom. *Be sure of this*, he says, or it could be the indicative 'you know this'; and for emphasis two verbs of knowing are used in the Greek. They had been taught this from their first hearing of the Christian gospel, but they must *Let no one deceive* them. There were then, as there always are, those who made light of sin, and scoffed at the thought of its consequences; but perhaps Paul was writing in the particular realization that among his readers were those representatives of early Gnosticism who said that the sins of the flesh were irrelevant to the spiritual life, and those too who took freedom from the law to mean liberty to continue in sin of any kind (*cf.* Rom. 6:1). The words of such, he would insist, were *empty words*. The word of God is solemn and true. 'No one given to fornication or indecency, or the greed which makes an idol of gain, has any share in the kingdom of Christ and of God' (NEB). Only by the forsaking of sin in true repentance is the way open by faith for people to have *inheritance* in God's *kingdom*. Otherwise, *because of these things* people remain 'children of disobedience' (AV) rather than children of God (see on 2:2), 'children of wrath' (2:3) rather than inheritors of God's kingdom by grace. Apart from the gift of forgiveness, men and women stand under *the wrath of God* because of sin, subject to his judgment, which in part is a present fact in that they are even now excluded from the life of God (*cf.* Rom. 1:18-32), but in greater part waits for that day when all stand before their Lord and judge.

In the naming of particular sins, we have essentially the same words as in verse 3, and the same connection of the word for 'covetous' or 'greedy' with sexual immorality. There, is, however, the further equation of this sin of 'greed' with idolatry (*cf.* Col. 3:5). For passion, whether for money or for sexual indulgence, is in effect putting an idol and object of desire and worship before God. To the Jew idolatry was the worst of sins, and perhaps Bruce (*EE*) is right in saying that 'The part which the commandment against covetousness played in Paul's own spiritual experience (Rom. 7:7ff.) no doubt made him acutely aware of the special deadliness of this subtle sin'. The solemn warning of judgment that is connected here with the 'sins of the flesh' raises certain questions in the minds of many. Are these sins worse than all others? Is it implied that sexual sin is the unforgivable sin, that debars one irrevocably from the kingdom of God? The very similar Pauline passages, 1 Corinthians 6:9–11 and Colossians 3:5–7, answer the second question. Paul could tell his readers that some of them had been guilty of these sins once, but now they were made new, pardoned, cleansed. Indeed we cannot say that these sins are viewed in the New Testament as worse than the sins of pride and subtler forms of self-centredness. But neither Law nor Prophets in the Old Testament, nor Gospels nor Letters in the New Testament, allow people to regard lightly the sins that break the bonds of marriage, destroy the sanctity of the family, and cause children to be brought to birth without parents to be responsible for their nurture and training. Finally, a word should be said on the form of the expression *the kingdom of Christ and of God*. God's kingdom is Christ's kingdom. Christ is not explicitly called God, but in the construction here the two are included under the one definite article in such a way that, as Westcott puts it, they are brought 'into a connexion incompatible with a simply human view of the Lord's Person (comp. Tit. ii:13; 2 Pet. 1:1)'.

7. *Therefore*, in the light of God's judgment and of the incompatibility of such sins with membership in the kingdom of God, Paul calls on his readers not to *associate with them*; and the word 'refers to participation, not just asssociation' (Stott). To be 'partners with them' (NIV) would be an utter denial of their Christian profession.

8. At this point Paul brings in one of the most common and most striking New Testament illustrations of the absoluteness of the difference between the old heathen life and the life 'in Christ'. 'God is light' (1 Jn. 1:5). Light expresses his majesty and glory (1 Tim. 6:16) and his perfect holiness, but also the truth that he wills to reveal himself to humanity (Ps. 43:3). The opposite of that glory and holiness and wisdom of God is darkness, and the world estranged from God dwells in such darkness (see on 1:18). Those who have found life 'in Christ' are essentially people who have been transferred from the realm of darkness to the realm of light (Acts 26:18; Rom. 13:12; 2 Cor. 4:6; Col. 1:13; 1 Pet. 2:9). Both in the Acts of the Apostles and in the Letters we can see the great part that this symbolism played in the preaching and teaching of the early church and of Paul in particular.

The special point to be noticed here is that he does not simply say, 'You were in darkness before'; there was indeed some light in the world around them, as God had not left himself without a witness. He says rather that 'darkness was . . . in them' (Abbott). *You were darkness*, he says. Their lives, and not just their environment, were dark. *But now*, he continues, *you are light in the Lord.* He says in effect, 'If you are in the Lord you are in the light and the light is in you.' They had received the light and become luminous themselves (*cf.* Mt. 5:14). Again the apostle's command is, 'Be what you are. You have become light. You are *children of light*, those whose very nature is light.' They are to pursue their daily lives in accordance with this new nature given to them in Christ, and to express this most effectively the apostle once again uses the word *walk* (see on 2:2). In the light that illuminates the pathway of God's will, and with light in their hearts, and radiating forth from their lives, they are to go on life's journey.

9. The same thing can be described in another way as bearing *the fruit of light*. This reading, accepted by all the recent versions, has better MS authority than the AV 'fruit of the Spirit', though the earliest authority we have for Ephesians (the Chester Beatty papyrus) favours the AV reading and thus indicates that the change to 'Spirit' must have been made very early. Paul may not be consciously thinking of the light as the seed planted in the life, and in due course having fruit there, but rather of the way that 'Christian virtues . . . grow naturally and spontaneously' and do not come 'by obedience to a book of rules' (Caird). RSV replaces the abstract nouns of the Greek by adjectives rendering *all that is good and right and true*. Many passages speak of 'righteousness' as a fruit of the life in Christ (*e.g.* Rom. 6:20–22; Phil. 1:11; Heb. 12:11). All that is corrupt and unjust in human relationships (see on 4:24) must have no place. Then instead of 'all malice' (4:31) there is to be 'all goodness' (NIV), the active seeking of good in every part of life. There is an instructive distinction between 'goodness' and 'righteousness' in Romans 5:7, showing that the former adds to moral uprightness and integrity the attractiveness of a beautiful character. Then, when the darkness of ignorance and blindness, error and deceit goes (4:14, 17–18, 22), there is 'truth' (AV, NIV) as the fruit of the light Christ brings.

10. Their life as children of light, moreover, was to involve a learning of *what is pleasing to the Lord*. Verse 9 is parenthetical, and so this is connected closely with verse 8. In the matter of daily life and decisions they had to find out and act on the will of God, *to learn* by doing. The thought is to be developed further in verse 17. The participle here (*dokimazontes*) is from a verb that sometimes means 'approving' (as in Rom. 14:22 and 1 Cor. 16:3), but more commonly 'proving' (AV) for oneself. It indicates the demand for careful thought and discrimination. The light of God is given, but it does not free us from the responsibility of thought and choice. Romans 12:2 is most closely similar to this as it speaks of proving 'what is the will of God, what is good and acceptable and perfect'. The word there translated 'acceptable' is the same Greek word *euarestos* that we have here better rendered by the more personal *pleasing* to the Lord. The desires and choices of those who walk in the light are governed by their prior determination, to please not themselves (Gal. 1:10), but their Lord (2 Cor. 5:9; Phil 4:18; Col. 1:10).

11–13. The old life that was *darkness* was essentially *unfruitful* (*cf.* Rom. 6:21). The apostle does not set one kind of fruit over against another. It is a matter of fruit or no fruit in the sight of God; wheat or tares; a harvest of good, or merely works – the endless, strenuous but futile human striving instead of the natural development of the life of God within that leads to its outward manifestation in ways which are a blessing to all (Gal. 5:16–23). Since the *darkness* has been banished by the coming of the light, Christians must *Take no part in* the old. The injunction of verse 7 is thus repeated.

The responsibility of the Christian with regard to the works of the ungodly is *instead* to *expose them*. The verb *elenchō* is one that has a wide range of meaning, and so the context must help to guide us for its interpretation here. Originally it meant to 'disgrace' or 'put to shame'; then it had the sense of examining in order to reprove or convict, and so also to 'bring to the proof' or to 'confute' (LS). The New Testament speaks of people being convicted by the law (Jas. 2:9), by conscience (Jn. 8:9), and by the working of the Spirit (Jn. 16:8). This is not quite the meaning here. Nor can it be simply 'reprove' (AV), as it clearly is in Luke 3:19, and in such passages as 1 Timothy 5:20 and Titus 2:15, where it is shown that the Christian leader's duty is to rebuke specific sins. For the next verse here (in a way similar to v. 3) continues, *For it is a shame even to speak of the things that they do in secret*. So the meaning is that the Christian, by a life so essentially different from those around him, rather than by reproof in speech, is to *expose* their sins. (*Cf.* Wisdom of Solomon 2:14–15) 'Paul's idea is that of a silent process, comparable to the action of light' (Scott). The use of the word, and the whole thought of the passage, is similar to that of John 3:20. As light shows up that which is filthy, so the life (and not just the words) of the person who has come to be light in the Lord (v. 8) shows up 'the barren deeds of darkness, . . . for what they are' (NEB).

The apostle thinks of the work of grace in the lives of those who do not believe, in three stages – they are exposed, they allow themselves to be manifested, and then they become light. In the beginning their shameful deeds are done in darkness – 'they neither see their own baseness, nor think that it is seen by God' (Calvin). But then the light of Christ, shining from the lives of those who have come to know him, breaks in. Such a coming of the light involves a crisis of judgment (Jn. 3:19–21). If people hate the light, they will try to avoid it, and shun the exposing of their works. But if they allow their lives to be exposed for what they are, they are *exposed by the light* (*cf.* 1 Cor. 14:24–25). Their whole lives can then be brought to Christ; and when people are prepared to submit to his scrutiny and dealing, then in his mercy they become *light*. The darkness is swept away 'and everything thus illuminated is all light' (NEB). This is the goal, as verse 8 has put it already – men and women not only receive the light, but become luminous. Such is the work of Christian evangelism, the light of one soul making another light. The AV translation 'whatsoever doth make manifest is light' depends on taking the participle (*phaneroumenon*) as a middle voice, which is without parallel in the New Testament, and particularly unlikely here as the same form has just been used for the passive, and the passive in fact gives a much stronger sense to the whole passage.

14. There follows now a relevant quotation, the substance of which is scriptural (Is. 9:2; 26:19; 52:1; 60:1), but whose words do not correspond precisely to the Old Testament. Their form (in that they refer to the work of *Christ*) prevents our thinking that they might be an otherwise unrecorded saying of the Lord himself. The most likely explanation is that we have here another little fragment of an early Christian hymn (see on v. 19). It might well be from a baptismal hymn, since coming to Christ and being baptized were spoken of as enlightenment (*cf.* Heb. 6:4; 10:32). 'It is significant' also, Bruce (*EE*) points out, that the 'precise rhythm' used here 'was specially asssociated with religious initiation-chants', so that there is some real possibility in the suggestion that 'Christians took the rhythm over for use in the act of Christian initiation'. In it three metaphors for turning to God are linked – awaking from sleep, being raised *from the dead*, and going out of the darkness into the *light*. The challenge to *Awake* from the sleep of carelessness and sin comes similarly in Romans 13:11, the passage that led to Augustine's conversion (*cf.* 1 Thes. 5:6–7). The beginning of chapter 2 has already described sin as spiritual death, and shown that Christ's gift is nothing less than new life. The symbolism of light and darkness is the dominant theme of these verses. The verb used here is *epiphaūo*, equivalent to *epiphauskō*, used in the Septuagint of Job 25:5 and 31:26 of the sun or moon shining forth, and to *epiphōskō* used in Matthew 28:1 and Luke 23:54 of the new day dawning. So it is best to take it as the NIV, 'Christ will shine on you'.

D. WISDOM TO REPLACE FOLLY (5:15–21)

15. The apostle has spoken of the sins of the heathen life which must be renounced, and in doing so he has spoken of forsaking the darkness of that old life, and coming to be light in the Lord. But light is a symbol of knowledge as well as of purity. In Christ his readers have been enlightened. So they must live – again the word *walk* is used (see on 2:2) – day by day, *not as unwise . . . but as wise*. Wisdom has been given (1:8), and they can pray in all things for the spirit of wisdom (1:17). So they must display in their lives the wisdom of God (3:10). As the context shows, and as Paul puts it in the parallel in Colossians 4:5 – 'Conduct yourselves wisely toward outsiders' – his particular thought was of their life before the eyes of the non-Christian world. The AV 'walk circumspectly' is probably not correct here. In different MSS the adverb *akribōs* is in different positions. AV translates those MSS where it is next to the verb *walk* and after the conjunction *pōs* (RV 'how'). The more likely reading is that which has it before the conjunction, and thus we have RSV, *Look carefully then how you walk*, and Moffat, 'Be strictly careful then about the life you lead'. 'He bids them keep a close watch on the principles by which they are regulating their lives' (Murray). This is a command that is essentially more likely to come from Paul's pen than that they should walk 'precisely' or 'strictly'. Paul could well use this word in its superlative form of his former life as a Pharisee (Acts 26:5), but to use it of the Christian life would have conveyed too much of a suggestion of renewed legalism.

16. Once again he is very practical. Walking in wisdom involves in particular the right use of *time*, and not just the space of time to work for God that each day offers (for which the Gk. *chronos* would have been used), but the fit time, the God-given opportunity (*kairos* – see on 1:10). Galatians 6:10 is parallel, 'as we have opportunity, let us do good to all men'. 'Making the most of every opportunity' NIV translates our verse here. The verb used is *exagorazō*, meaning literally 'buying from'. It has the sense of 'redeem' in Galatians 3:13 and 4:5, but the prefix *ex-* may have simply an intensive force, and perhaps the word has lost its connections with marketing, and simply means 'Use . . . to the full' (NEB). Paul adds the reminder that *the days are evil*, and so shows he is aware of the great pressure in the direction of misuse of time and opportunity. Christians must not relax but overcome that pressure in their own lives and use every chance to turn others from darkness to light. There may also be the suggestion that *because the days are evil*, they are under God's judgment, and for that reason 'the time is short' (1 Cor. 7:29, AV), and each opportunity must be taken before it is too late. As Caird puts it, 'the old order was already tottering to its doom under the weight of its own corruption.'

17. He repeats that they must *not be foolish*, this time using *aphrones*, a word that suggests not so much a lack of essential wisdom (as does *asophoi* in v. 15) as a moral stupidity in action. Their earnest quest each day, if they are to buy up their opportunities, is to have 'understanding' (AV), and that not in any merely theoretical way; the most vital thing to be understood is *what the will of the Lord is*. To know that *will of the Lord* is in God's plan for all (*cf.* Acts 22:14); therefore such knowledge is to be sought more than any other knowledge. Verse 10 has already spoken of trying 'to learn what is pleasing to the Lord'. Romans 12:2, as we have seen, combines both expressions in saying 'that you may prove what is the will of God, what is good and acceptable and perfect'. Thus Paul repeatedly presents this seeking to know, understand and thus to do the will of God as a priority for the Christian's daily walk.

18. A particular and indeed prominent manifestation of the folly of the old life is drunkenness. Right down the ages, as literature from the earliest period onwards bears testimony, people have sought to rise above their cares and gain a sense of exhilaration and gaiety through intoxicants. Scripture never demands total abstinence from intoxicants (except for those who had taken special vows). That must be a question left to the individual conscience, but the Bible often speaks against drunkenness. It was a danger in the church of New Testament days, even among those who might be chosen as leaders, as 1 Timothy 3:3, 8 and Titus 1:7 and 2:3 show. The specific objection here to being *drunk with wine* is that it involves *debauchery*. The word *asōtia* involves not only the uncontrolled action of the drunken man (*cf.* the use of the word in Tit. 1:6 and 1 Pet. 4:4), but also the idea of wastefulness. Hence NEB 'dissipation'. The corresponding adverb is used in the familiar phrase 'riotous living' in the parable of the prodigal son (Lk. 15:13, AV). Both the wastefulness and the lack of self-control implied by this word are things which should not be seen in the lives of those who have found in Christ the source and the way of wisdom.

But again the apostle is not merely negative. He does not seek simply to take away joys and pleasures from people's lives. He would replace them by higher joys and better pleasures. It is no mere coincidence that in Acts 2 also the fullness of wine and the fullness of the Spirit are set side by side. There is the implication there, repeated here, that the Christian knows a better way than by wine of being lifted above the depression and the joyless monotony of life, a better way of removing self-consciousness and quickening thought and word and action than by the use of intoxicants. It is by being *filled with the Spirit*.

There is a certain strangeness about the construction in the Greek here that led the RV to give the alternative translation in the margin, 'be filled in spirit'. Usually the Greek New Testament has the genitive case after the verb or adjective used to describe the filling of the Holy Spirit. (This is the case in Acts 2:4; 4:31; 9:17; 11:24 and 13:52.) The preposition 'in' (Gk. *en*) is unusual, though not impossible, as Acts 1:5 shows when it speaks of being baptized 'in the Holy Ghost' (RV mg.). Romans 8:9 speaks of being 'in the Spirit' to describe the Christian's experience, as against the non-Christian's life which is still 'in the flesh'. Ephesians, moreover, gives a special significance to this phrase 'in the Spirit' (see also 2:18, 22; 3:5; 6:18, in the Gk.) as well as to 'in Christ'. It is as if the two thoughts of being *filled with the Spirit*, and living a life 'in the Spirit' (see on 2:18), are being expressed at the same time; and this may be assisted by the fact that the little preposition *en* in the New Testament can often have a meaning equivalent to *with*, and also by *en* being used with the relative in the preceding clause. To take the expression as meaning merely to be filled in spirit would be to deprive it of the force of meaning that it clearly has in the context, and indeed how can the Christian be filled in spirit but by the Holy Spirit of God? Finally the tense of the verb, present imperative in the Greek, should be noted, implying as it does that the experience of receiving the Holy Spirit so that every part of life is permeated and controlled by him is not a 'once for all' experience. In the early chapters of the Acts of the Apostles it is repeated a number of times that the same apostles were 'filled with the Holy Spirit' (*e.g.* Acts 2:4; 4:31). The practical implication is that Christians are to keep their lives open to be filled constantly and repeatedly by the divine Spirit. So NEB 'let the Holy Spirit fill you'.

19. Instead of the expression of drunkenness in *asōtia*, there should be an exhilaration of the Spirit expressed in song and praise. In the light of the sequence of this verse it has been suggested that the drunkenness referred to was a feature even of Christian assemblies (1 Cor. 11:20–21 is compared). But neither the drunkenness nor the use of song need be given such a limitation. When the verse speaks of Christians *addressing one another* in such a way the thought is that the fullness of the Spirit will find manifestation in fellowship whenever Christians are found together, and will be given joyful expression in song and praise. The *psalmos* was originally that which was sung to the harp, and here perhaps includes not only the *psalms* of the Old Testament, but those (like Lk. 1:46–55, 68–79 and 2:29–32) which were songs of the new, but in the spirit and manner of the old psalms. The *hymnos* in classical Greek was a festive lyric in praise of a god or hero. We have already seen in this letter possible evidence of early Christian *hymns* (4:4–6 and 5:14), and we may have other such fragments in 1 Timothy 1:17; 2:5–6; 6:15–16; 2 Timothy 2:11–13; and Revelation 4:11; 5:13 and 7:12. It is doubtful whether we should press a distinction between the *hymns* and *spiritual songs*. Every expression of Christian joy is welcomed, and all should come from the *heart* – in fact the *melody* may sometimes be in the heart and not expressed in sound – and go forth addressed *to the Lord*. A number of New Testament passages like this (*e.g.* Acts 16:25; 1 Cor. 14:26; Col. 3:16; Jas. 5:13) indicate the place of song in the early church; in the second century Pliny and Tertullian give the same testimony. *Singing* has always had a great place in the church's life and worship, and every new movement of the Spirit has brought a fresh outbust of song.

20. Whether in song or in other ways the Christian, the apostle instructs, should constantly be *giving thanks.* Repeatedly, as we have seen (on 1:16), he gives this instruction, and his own writings, as doubtless all his life, are an example in this. The injunction to give thanks *always and for everything* 'presupposes a deep underlying faith that God can produce good out of even the most unpromising situation, and that thankfulness, therefore, can be felt because of the confident hope that in some wonderful way God will make even disaster and suffering an occasion for later blessing' (Mitton, *NCB*). We may compare Paul's attitude of thanksgiving even in weaknesses and afflictions and persecutions, shown in such passages as 2 Corinthians 11:18ff., and 12:5–10. *God the Father* is the source of all blessing, and thus himself to be blessed (*cf.* 1:3), but this is rightly *in the name of our Lord Jesus Christ* because every blessing comes to us through him, and our praise and thanksgiving go to the Father through him and in his name.

21. In this verse there is an unexpected, but not illogical, turn in the apostle's exhortation, and one that leads him into the instructions that follow in the whole of the next section, 5:22 – 6:9. He has implied in verse 19 that the enthusiasm that the Spirit inspires is not to be expressed individualistically, but in fellowship. He has seen the dangers of individualism in a Christiarr community, and in 1 Corinthians 14:26–33 he corrects this (*cf.* also Phil. 2:1ff. and 4:2). He knew from experience that the secret of maintaining joyful fellowship in the community was the order and discipline that come from the willing submission of one person to another (*cf.* Eph. 4:2–3). Pride of position and the authoritarian spirit are destructive of fellowship. The importance to Paul of the whole concept of submission is evident from the use of the word more than twenty times in his letters. He is to apply this in special instances in the next section, but we should note that he first gives it a completely general application. There must be a willingness in the Christian fellowship to serve any, to learn from any, to be corrected by any, regardless of age, sex, class, or any other division.

Undoubtedly the true reading here, though the phrase is unique in the New Testament, is *out of reverence for Christ* rather than the AV 'in the fear of God'. 'The fear of the Lord' is a great principle of life enunciated again and again in the Old Testament. For Christians this remains unchanged (2 Cor. 7:1; 1 Pet. 2:17), but they know God in Christ, are called to Christ's discipleship, and their whole life is 'in Christ'. So all human relationships, as Paul will now show, find their pattern and meaning and ordered expression under the authority of Christ (*cf.* 2 Cor. 4:5), and, as Masson stresses, remembering that Christ made himself the servant of all (Mk. 10:45). The most vital of these relationships are those of the family, for in every age the home must be the place, where, above all, the peace and harmony, the love and discipline of Christ are most clearly manifest.

V. RELATIONSHIPS (5:22 – 6:9)

A. HUSBANDS AND WIVES (5:22–33)

22. Codes of household duties were familiar to the Greeks from Aristotle onwards; they became a familiar part of Christian instruction, as is realized by comparing this whole section with Colossians 3:18 – 4:1 and 1 Peter 2:18 – 3:7. In dealing with personal relationships, Paul begins with that which is basic for the home, between husbands and wives. It is significant that throughout this section husbands and wives are reminded of their duties and not their rights. It is important also to read all that is said in this section realizing both that it follows what has been said in verse 21 about mutual submission and that it presupposes what is stated in Galatians 3:28 of the equality in Christ of male and female. In the Christian family, however, as Paul sees it there is order and *wives* are called to *be subject to* their *husbands* (*cf.* 1 Cor. 11:3; Col. 3:18; Tit. 2:5; 1 Pet. 3:1–2). There is no verb in the Greek original here, but the whole structure of the verse depends on the participle in verse 21. The New Testament throughout emphasizes the dignity of womanhood, and it is an indisputable fact that the example and teaching of Christ have lifted women in one country and society after another to a position that they did not occupy before. Whereas in many great religions, not least in Judaism and Islam, women have a far lower place than men, the New Testament emphasizes their spiritual equality (Gal. 3:28). Moreover, as we see most notably in 1 Corinthians 7:3–5, Paul also 'pleads for a true mutuality in the physical sex relation' (Allan). Equality as persons and submission to one another are basic Christian principles in the husband-wife relationship. As J. H. Yoder well puts it, there is no 'difference in worth' but in the family, for its order and its unity, there must be leadership, and the responsibility of leadership is that of the husband and father.[1] When the apostle adds the little phrase *as to the Lord*, he does not imply that the relationship of wife to husband is directly comparable to her relationship to her heavenly Lord, but rather that when a duty is performed 'in the Lord' (as the parallel passage in Col. 3:18 puts it), it is carried out 'as is fitting in the Lord'. (See also 6:1 and 5.)

23–24. The man's place in the family is one of leadership, to be qualified by the highest demand for love in the verses that follow. But the apostle does much more than present the wife's duty as one to be carried out 'as to the Lord' (v. 22). Husband and wife are to see their relationship as following the patterns of the relationship between Christ and his church. *The husband is the head of the wife as Christ is the head of the church.* In the rest of the section the apostle uses one to illustrate the other, backwards and forwards. He uses the marriage relationship to illustrate the deep spiritual relationship of love and dependence, of authority and obedience, between Christ and his church. As Allan puts it, 'Marriage supplies an image of the relationship of the Church to Christ more adequate than the image of the Temple to its Foundation Stone, or even than the image of the Body and its Head. Here we pass from imagery taken from the inanimate or the biological realm to imagery taken from the most fully personal realm.' There is, of course,

---

[1] J. H. Yoder, *The Politics of Jesus* (Grand Rapids, 1972), p. 185.

an Old Testament background to this in the way that the prophets regarded the Lord as husband of his people, entering into a marriage covenant with them, and loving them with steadfast love, even when, because of their idolatry, they were like an unfaithful wife who had committed adultery (*e.g.* Is. 54:1–8; 62:4–5; Je. 3:6–14; 31:32; Ezk. 16; 23; Ho. 1 – 3). Our Lord in his parables used and extended the application of the same analogy (*e.g.* Mt. 9:15; 22:2–13; 25:1–10). On the other hand the marriage relationship is infinitely ennobled by its comparison with the relationship between Christ and his church. There has been much scholarly discussion of the biblical meaning of *head* and in some studies stress has been placed on the *head* as 'source'[1] rather than 'leader'. In 4:15–16 Christ is spoken of as 'the head . . . from whom the whole body' grows; Christ 'enables the church to grow; he knits her into a unity; he nourishes her by caring for each member; he gives her strength to build herself up in love' (Barth, *AB*). We can understand that as involved here, and the concept of 'source' is present in Gn. 2:18–24, but from the present context, as from other uses of the word (*e.g.* 1:22; Col. 1:18; 2:10), it would be hard to remove the concept of leadership.

The apostle, however, cannot limit himself to this description of the relation of Christ to his church, as *head* of the *body*. He must add further that Christ *is himself its Saviour*. Perhaps he wishes to imply that there are limitations to the analogy that he has just presented. In the light of the following verses, however, we may ask whether he is not rather beginning to express another part of the analogy. The sacrificial concern of the Lord for the salvation of the church should have a parallel, even if at a much lower level, in the loving and sacrificial concern of the husband for the welfare of his wife. He is 'the protector of his wife' (Bruce, *EE*).

But before this point is developed, he would stress again the wife's duty. It needs no argument that *the church is subject to Christ*; even *so* then, he says, *let wives also be subject to their husbands*. The final addition *in everything* might seem more than

---

[1] See W. Grudem, 'Does *kephalē* ["head"] mean "source" or "authority over" in Greek Literature? A survey of 2,336 examples', Appendix 1, in G. W. Knight III, *The Role Relationship of Men and Women – New Testament Teaching* (Moody Press, Chicago, ²1985), pp. 49–80. Grudem finds no clear evidence for "source" as a legitimate meaning for *kephalē*.

can be accepted as God's purpose by this present generation with its stress on the emancipation of womanhood, and the place of woman outside the home in every sphere of life that man occupies. Has not a woman equal rights with a man to self-determination? May not a married woman make herself a career just as much as her husband? The answer that the New Testament would give is that she may do so, provided that it does not mean the sacrifice of the divine pattern for home life, for family relationships and for the whole Christian community. She may fulfil any function and any responsibility in society, but if she has accepted before God the responsibility of marriage and of a family, these must be her first concern, and this is expressed here in terms of her relationship to her husband as head of the home. 'As the Church wholeheartedly devotes herself to Christ, so the wife wholeheartedly accepts her place in the family and devotes herself without reserve to fulfil her function as wife and mother' (Allan). *Subject to* her husband *in everything* does not mean, however, that she is in the hands of one who has authority to command what he pleases. He is one whose duty to her is expressed in nothing short of the highest demand of self-giving love. Her subjection in the light of this, and in the light of the high ideal of unity that is to be expressed in verses 28–31, is such that 'she can never find grievous or humiliating' (Allan). The husband's commitment to his wife and to home responsibilities is certainly no less demanding than that asked of the wife – but the two are different, and complementary.

25. Now the apostle turns to address *husbands*. Chrysostom puts it, 'Hast thou seen the measure of obedience? hear also the measure of love. Wouldst thou that thy wife should obey thee as the Church doth Christ? have care thyself for her, as Christ for the Church.' The quality of the love that husbands are required to give to their wives is first shown by the word that is used for *love*. Three other words might have been used in Greek for the love of husband for wife, and classical writers would more naturally have used them. There was the word *eraō* that expressed the deep sexual passion of man for woman, and the words *phileō* and *storgeō* were used for affection within the family. None of these is used here; instead Paul chooses the typically Christian word *agapaō, love* that is totally unselfish, that seeks not its own satisfaction, nor even affection answering affection, but that strives for the highest good of the one loved. This love has as its standard and model the love of Christ for his church. 'It means not only a practical concern for the welfare of the other, but a continual readiness to subordinate one's own pleasure and advantage for the benefit of the other. It implies patience and kindliness, humility and courtesy, trust and support (1 Cor. 13:4–7). This love means that one is eager to understand what the needs and interests of the other are, and will do everything in his power to supply those needs and further those interests' (Mitton, *NCB*).

26–27. Typically, Paul cannot refer to what Christ has done in love for his church without amplifying it. Christ gave himself even to the death of the cross *that he might sanctify* and cleanse his church. Such was the purpose of his sacrifice. We often distinguish between justification as an act and sanctification as a process. Sometimes the New Testament may permit this. The tense of the participle here, translated accurately by RSV *having cleansed*, might suggest this in the present instance – first cleansing, then sanctification – but in fact the first verb is an aorist in the Greek, indicating a single act rather than a continuing experience. A number of times in the New Testament sanctification is spoken of as an act accomplished in the past as much as justification or forgiveness (*cf.* 1 Cor. 1:2; 6:11; 2 Tim. 2:21; Heb. 10:29). The two words used here describe two aspects of the same experience; Christ's work is to 'cleanse from the old, and consecrate to the new', and 'in time the two are coincident' (Robinson).

Two agencies are described as making possible the cleansing. It is *by the washing of water*, and it is *with the word*. How does *the washing of water*, the Christian sacrament of baptism, help to effect sanctification, and the cleansing of the heart from sin? The two are connected again in Titus 3:5. Calvin no doubt gives the true meaning when he says, 'Having mentioned the inward and hidden sanctification, he now adds the outward symbol, by which it is visibly confirmed; as if he had said that a pledge of that sanctification is held out to us by baptism.' Any thought of the external rite itself automaticaly conveying the inward spiritual grace is excluded by the addition of *with the word*. It is probably the word of the gospel (*cf.* Rom. 10:8; 1 Pet. 1:25) rather than the human 'pledge' (Bruce) or 'confession' of faith (Moffatt) or the 'baptismal formula' (Schlier) that is meant. Such is the means by which the sanctification becomes effective in people's lives, and that only as it is believed. As John 15:3 and 17:17 express it, the word received cleanses and sanctifies. The apostle is using great economy of words, and it may be that in every expression he has the analogy of marriage in mind. Here there may be an implied reference to the ceremonial bath taken by a bride before marriage. There is also a Jewish custom that may go back even to those days, by which, at the giving of the ring, the bridegroom said, 'Behold, thou art sanctified to me' (see Murray).

There is a more obvious way in which an analogy can be drawn between marriage and what Christ seeks to do for his church. The reader is called to think of the preparations that a bride makes for her marriage that she may appear before her husband in all her beauty. She wants to be seen lovely and *in splendour, without spot or wrinkle or any such thing*. So the church is to appear before her heavenly bridegroom (*cf.* Rev. 21:2). But the difference in this case is that she can do nothing of herself to make herself beautiful in the eyes of her Lord. Of necessity it is all his work. He must thus *present the church to himself*. The word translated *in splendour* (*endoxon*) speaks of honour, of glory, of beauty, but it is implied that the church owes 'all her glory to His work' (Moule, *CB*). She can only be *without spot or wrinkle*, the stains of sin, and the decadence of age, through what is effected by his sanctifying and renewing work. Paul makes further use of the phrase he has used in 1:4, *holy and without blemish*. This is the object of our Lord's cleansing work; indeed in chapter 1 it is spoken of as the whole purpose and goal of the work of Christ. It is the goal that Paul kept before him in his own ministry. In 2 Corinthians 11:2 he speaks of his 'divine jealousy' over the church to 'present' her 'as a pure bride' to Christ. In Colossians 1:28 he speaks similarly of his work, not simply in terms of bringing people to the knowledge of their salvation, but of presenting all perfect in Christ Jesus.[1]

---

[1] Barth, *AB*, vol. 2, pp. 668–699, has a valuable and detailed note on biblical and extra-biblical background for what is said in these verses about bride and bridegroom.

28–29. Thus the thought and argument go back and forth. The love of husbands for their wives is to be modelled on the love of Christ for his church. The love of Christ and his desire for his church are pictured in the preparation of a bride for her husband. Now he goes on, *so husbands should love their wives*. Though there is a uniqueness in the application of verses 26–27 to the work of Christ for his church, yet there seems inevitably the hint that, even if at an incomparably lower level, the husband is to love his wife, not just because of the beauty he finds in her, but to make her more beautiful. Christ sees the church in all her weaknesses and failures, and yet loves her as his body, and seeks her true sanctification. *Even so husbands* are to *love their wives as their own bodies*. It would seem that Genesis 2:24 is already in mind, though it is not quoted till verse 31. And when he says *He who loves his wife loves himself*, he is not exhorting the husband to love his wife as an extension of self-love, or because it is to his own advantage. Again the word *agapaō*, used for *love*, shows that this is not the case. A man should seek his own highest spiritual welfare, and so the highest good of his wife in every way, as united with himself in the marriage bond. His wife is not a person lower in social status, much less one over whom he has rights of ownership, but a part of himself.

Paul develops this a little further, and comes closer to the terms of Genesis 2:24 when he says, *For no man ever hates his own flesh*. A man's wife, as Moule puts it, is 'in a profound and sacred sense, part and parcel of his own living frame' (*CB*). A man *nourishes and cherishes* his own body, Paul says, employing words that he uses in 6:4 and in 1 Thessalonians 2:7 for the nurture of children, and showing incidentally that he gives no place to asceticism for its own sake (*cf.* Col. 2:23). Such self-love is not wrong. It is the law of life, and the extension of it to similar care for one's life-partner is the law of marriage. But this thought of the intimate care and love that a husband owes and should give to his partner, Paul cannot help but apply back to what is perfectly and more wonderfully true of what *Christ does* for *the church*.

30. Now, dwelling simply on this spiritual analogy, he says, *because we are members of his body*. In 4:25 the thought is of

Christians being members 'one of another'; in 1:23 and 4:12 and 16 it is of the church as the body of which Christ is head. Here, though the words in the AV 'of his flesh, and of his bones' are probably not original, but added under the influence of Genesis 2:23, the context shows that the apostle's thought at this point is the still deeper one of the intimacy of the Christian's relationship with Christ. The members are part of him, as the branches are part of the vine in the teaching of John 15. As in the divine purpose the wife becomes part of the very life of her husband, and he nourishes and cherishes her, even so the Lord does to us as *members* of himself, part of his own life that he has joined to himself.

31. Now at last comes the quotation of Genesis 2:24 that has been influencing all the apostle's thought. This statement from the creation story is the most profound and fundamental statement in the whole of Scripture concerning God's plan for marriage. It has been the ultimate bulwark of the church against the arguments for allowing polygamy to remain in the societies where she has met it; it is the ultimate argument against promiscuity; it is the ultimate reason why the church can have no pleasure in the dissolution of marriage by divorce. When our Lord was questioned concerning the legal permission given to divorce he gave the answer that must still be given. In an imperfect society, in need of such laws, and 'For the hardness of people's hearts' (Mt. 19:8; Mk. 10:5), divorce may be allowed, but it is a decline from the divine purpose, and it can never be seen in any other light. The Lord gave no new teaching on the matter, but directed his appeal back to this verse (Mt. 19:3–9 and Mk. 10:2–12). Prior to marriage a man or a woman has his or her closest bond with parents, and to them has the greatest obligation. The new bond and obligation that marriage involves transcends the old. Filial duty does not cease, but the most intimate relationship now, and the highest loyalty, is that between husband and wife, and parents only imperil that relationship by trying in any way to come between. There must be a leaving of parents on the part of husband and wife, and a corresponding renouncing of rights on the part of parents. Then there is a cleaving of the two together in the 'one flesh' (AV) relationship, blessed by God and a comfort and blessing to both.

32. Paul himself, however, in his work as an apostle, was pre-occupied with the thought of the church prepared as a bride for her marriage, and living as a wife in love and unity and loyalty with her husband. He saw the beauty of the divine pattern and ideal for marriage, and he strove and exhorted husbands and wives to work out that pattern in the stuff of daily living. But to him in his own personal life and work it was above all the highest analogy that he knew for the still more wonderful relation of Christ and his church, to which he could not help returning again and again. There is literal truth, he would say, to be worked out in every home. But there is also a *mystērion*. This word we have seen used for the great eternal secret of God's purpose for mankind, hidden in the past but now revealed in Christ (see on 1:9 and see also 3:3–4, 9; 6:19). It is used more generally in the plural of divine truths (as in 1 Cor. 4:1; 13:2 and 14:2), but it is used sometimes in the singular, as here, to denote some particular deep truth of the divine plan which has been revealed (*cf.* Rom. 11:25; 1 Cor. 15:51). *This mystery is a profound one*, is the RSV translation. The sense is 'The truth that lies here, hidden but revealed in Christ, is a wonderful one'.[1] NEB gets it well, 'It is a great truth that is hidden here.' (1 Tim. 3:16 affords a close parallel to the expression at this point.) Nor should the words that conclude the verse be taken to imply that Paul had no thought of the literal application of Genesis 2:24. Westcott says that after speaking of the *mystērion*, 'St. Paul seems to pause for a while and contemplates the manifold applications of the primitive ordinance … and then he marks the greatest of all'. *I am saying that it refers to Christ and the church.* They are made one together. The husband's position as head, and his duty of sacrificial love and devoted care for his wife are but pictures, imperfect, but the best that this life can offer, of Christ as head, of his love, self-sacrifice and concern for his church. The dependence of the wife on her husband and her duty to accept his leadership are a picture of how the church should live and act towards her divine Lord.

---

[1] The Latin translation of *mystērion* as *sacramentum* has led to marriage being regarded as a sacrament, but in the usual sense we give to the word 'sacramentum', it can hardly be so called, or set alongside the two great 'sacraments of the gospel'.

33. However the last word must be the practical one on the subject that the apostle had set out to write about. Leaving aside now the analogy to which he has been led, he sums up, *let each one of you love his wife as himself.* Love, pure and simple, but transcendent, the truly Christian love (*agapē*) that embraces what is pure in every other love, is the husband's duty. *Let the wife see that she respects her husband.* Respect is the wife's duty. The verb here is more literally 'fear' (RV), the same as the noun in verse 21, but that word conjures up in our minds the thought of fearfulness, which is far removed from the true meaning here. Love cannot co-exist with such fearfulness (see 1 Jn. 4:18), but a deep strong love of wife for husband can be based only on the 'fear' that is both 'reverence' (AV) and 'respect'. It is this kind of 'fear' that the Bible so frequently calls on every individual soul to show before God (see on v. 21), and which finds special human application too in the duty of children to parents (Lv. 19:3), subjects to their rulers (Jos. 4:14; Pr. 24:21), servants to masters (1 Pet. 2:18), and now here wives to husbands.

B. CHILDREN AND PARENTS (6:1–4)

1. From the relationship of wives and husbands the apostle now turns to that between children and their parents. *Children* are first called to *obey* their *parents.* Both here and in Colossians 3:20 the 'honour' of the fifth commandment is given the specific direction of obedience. Then in a manner typical of this letter the apostle adds the phrase *in the Lord.* Its use here is not because the apostle contemplates 'the situation where parental orders might be contrary to the law of Christ' (Bruce, *EE*), but it is the Christian home which is in his mind. The Colossians parallel may be taken as interpretative when it says of such filial obedience, 'this pleases the Lord'. Even children, in their simple way, can know what it means to love *in the Lord*, and to *obey* for his sake. Then the reason given for obedience is striking in its austerity: *for this is right.* Perhaps his thought is that it is accepted as proper in every society; it is right by the Old Testament law; it is in accordance with the example of

Christ himself (Lk. 2:51). Or it may be that the form of his expression was intended to carry the reminder that in some things children must accept and follow before they can see all the reasons.

2. The fifth commandment is quoted, essentially as in the Septuagint of Exodus 20:12 and Deuteronomy 5:16. As Murray says, 'In the case of the children it was natural to clinch the instruction by a quotation from the Commandments which they must have been taught early.' But, despite his austere statement in verse 1, the apostle does not stop with stating the law that is to be obeyed. There is *a promise* attached to it. It is difficult, however, to be sure what he meant when he said that this fifth commandment *is the first commandment with a promise*. It is asked, Does not the second commandment contain a promise too? Or, if the reference there to the mercy of God being shown to thousands of generations is to be regarded as a statement rather than a promise, then is not the fifth the only one of the ten with a promise? Various explanations have been offered. Some have taken *first* to mean the first in the second table of the Decalogue. But the Jews commonly divided the Ten into two tables of *five* each. There is indeed no need to take the Decalogue as the sum total of the commandments. As Moule puts it, 'The Decalogue is, so to speak, the first page of the whole Law-Book of Revelation' (*CB*). Others take *first* as meaning the first to be learnt by children, and then the words *with a promise* are added as a reminder for their encouragement. Perhaps, however, especially as there is no article before the noun in the Greek, we should take the meaning as that this fifth commandment is a 'primary commandment'. Matthew 23:23 and Mark 12:28 speak thus in terms of commandments of prior importance, and it is noteworthy that in Leviticus 19:1ff. the call to holiness is followed by a statement of various commandments of which this stands first. Thus we take it that this commandment is urged on children as a priority for them, but also as holding out a great promise.

3. In the quotation of the promise there is clear dependence on Exodus 20:12 and Deuteronomy 5:16, but the reference to

'the land which the Lord your God gives you' is shortened by the omission of the qualifying clause which no longer applied as in Old Testament days. Thus it became more natural to translate *on the earth*. It is not necessary to take the promise in an individualistic sense, or as a literal promise of longevity. Although the singular pronoun was used in the original, it is doubtful if, even in Old Testament days, it was intended as a personal promise for those who showed filial piety. Then, as in any generation, it could be seen that the strength of family life, and the training of children to habits of order and obedience, were the means and the marks of the stability of a community or nation. When the bonds of family life break up, when respect for parents fails, the community becomes decadent and will not *live long*.

4. As in the case of husbands and wives, not all the obligation is on one side. Parents have their duties, and a warning is necessary for them, and probably when the word *Fathers* is used, both parents are in mind, as apparently is the case in Hebrews 11:23. *Do not provoke your children to anger* is the word for parents. The noun from the verb here, *parorgizō*, has been used in 4:26, and the verb itself is in Romans 10:19, quoting Deuteronomy 32:21. It is right for parents to demand obedience, but there must not be a 'capricious exercise of authority' (Robinson). Discipline is essential in the home; but not unnecessary rules and regulations and endless petty correction by which children are 'discouraged' (Col. 3:21). As NEB puts it, 'You . . . must not goad your children to resentment'. The positive duty is expressed in a word used already in 5:29 where it is translated 'nourishes'. The word was used originally of bodily nourishment, but came to be used for the nurture of the body, mind and soul. With its intensive preposition (*ek-*) before it, it suggests 'development by care and pains' (Moule, *CB*). 'Let them be fondly cherished', says Calvin. But all the time, foremost in the parents' minds, is to be not just the harmonious relationships of the home, or the happiness of the children, but their regard for the Lord. The, highest duty of parents is to *bring . . . up* their children *in the discipline and instruction of the Lord*. The two nouns repay closer study. The noun *paideia*, and its corresponding verb, may have the force of 'correcting' or 'chastening', as in 1

Corinthians 11:32, 2 Corinthians 6:9 and 2 Timothy 2:25, but may also have the positive meaning of 'instruction' (*e.g.* Tit. 2:12). *Discipline* is perhaps the best translation. *Nouthesia* is more specifically *instruction* or 'correction', and it is used of the purpose of the Old Testament in 1 Corinthians 10:11. In fact it is significant that both words are used to express the purpose of Scripture, and that in 2 Timothy 3:16 we find the only other use of *paideia* in the Pauline corpus. The NEB well translates 'give them the instruction, and the correction, which belong to a Christian upbringing'. *The discipline and instruction of the Lord* is that which the Lord is able to bring into the life of a child if parents do their work of teaching and training in the word of the Lord. This is the highest duty of Christian parents. As Dale puts it, 'parents should care more for the loyalty of their children to Christ than for anything besides, more for this than for their health, their intellectual vigour and brilliance, their material prosperity, their social position, their exemption from great sorrows and great misfortunes.'

C. SERVANTS AND MASTERS (6:5-9)

5-7. Lastly the apostle turns to the relationships between servants and masters. In justice to the original and its setting in the life of the time, it should of course be said that the apostle is still dealing with relationships within the family or household as he writes this section, and that he has in mind household *slaves*. As Bruce (*EE*) points out, in this letter and also in Colossians and 1 Peter 'the injunctions to slaves are more extended than those to masters, and are accompanied by special encouragements', probably thus reflecting 'the social structure of the churches addressed'. But although the numerous slaves who had come into the Christian fold were in the apostle's mind as he wrote these words, the principles of the whole section apply to employees and employers in every age, whether in the home, in business, or in the state. 'The attitude to work and the spirit demanded of masters and those under them are just as relevant in a free society as in a slave economy' (Allan). In the first place there is here another application of the principle of submission that is the keynote of this section. *Be obedient,* servants are told, and the same word is used as in verse 1 in the address to children. Paul's choice of phrase in calling them to render this obedience *to those who are* their *earthly masters* immediately brings to their minds the higher master who is Lord over this relationship. In every case the apostle goes further than we might expect with his demand for submission. Here he does so by adding the phrase *with fear and trembling.* Indeed the thought that dominates the whole section on relationships is that of submission 'out of reverence for Christ' (see 5:21); it is a matter of reverence and respect, not of being afraid or terrified. The parallel passage in Colossians 3:22 enjoins servants to render obedience 'fearing the Lord' (*cf.* 1 Pet. 2:18). Murray perhaps is right when he says that 'An element of "fear" enters into all relationships when their essential sacredness is realized.' That sacredness is expressed here (in a way that is paralleled in 5:22 and 6:1) by the phrase *as to Christ.* Whatever the Christian does is to be done as to the Lord (Rom. 14:7–9),and this is particularly true of the attitude of submission that he is to show towards others.

It means, moreover, the transformation of the Christian's entire standards of work and service into something totally different from the standards of the world. Work and service are to be rendered to an earthly master, as if they were being offered to the heavenly Lord himself. This would hardly have been easier to accomplish for one who, in Paul's day, was a slave against his will, than it would be for an employee today, with all the arguments based on materialistic concepts to face. But once again Paul does not merely present a high spiritual ideal and leave it there. He is searchingly practical. He demands that service be given *in singleness of heart.* Honesty of purpose and whole-hearted effort must characterize the Christian employee. The same word (*haplotēs*) is applied to both 'secular' work and to the 'spiritual' service of Christians; the New Testament uses it most frequently of liberality in Christian giving (Rom. 12:8; 2 Cor. 8:2; 9:11, 13) The Bible allows no distinction between sacred and secular. *Eye-service* is excluded, and here and in Colossians 3:22 a word seems to have been invented by the apostle to express his thought. NIV helpfully translates, 'Obey them not only to win their favour when their eye is on you . . .'. The ideal for Christians is for their daily work, seen or unseen by others, to be accepted as *the will of God*, rejoiced in, and done not by constraint or carelessly but because it is his will. Christian employees are *servants* – even slaves – not merely of earthly masters, but *of Christ*. So all *service* is to be rendered, the apostle repeats, *as to the Lord and not to men*. 'The conviction of the Christian workman is that every single piece of work he produces must be good enough to show to God' (Barclay). In everything the spirit of the work, and not merely the output as other people see it, is what matters – what is done is to be done *from the heart* and *with a good will*. Then people will give loyal service and give their very best to those over them whatever the attitude shown to them in return. In all of this we can see that Paul's concern was not so much for human rights, as for Christians to serve their Lord whole-heartedly whatever their situation in life might be.

8. Finally in these instructions to servants the eye is turned to the future reckoning. The New Testament often thus gives the double incentive. Worthy service is to be given as to the Lord who even now is witness of all that is done. But also it is to be remembered that *from the Lord* a person *will receive* again *whatever good*, or bad, he or she has done. Both good and bad are mentioned in the parallel Colossians 3:24–25, and in 2 Corinthians 5:10, and in the Lord's parables of judgment such as those in Matthew 25. But only *good* is mentioned here, since the apostle's purpose at this point is encouragement rather than warning. He knows what it will mean to his readers who are slaves to live out what he has said. So he reminds them that nothing is unwitnessed by the Lord in heaven, nothing well done is ever done in vain. There may be no thanks on earth. A person may reap only criticism and misunderstanding. But there is an unfailing reward for faithful service (*cf.* Lk. 6:35; 1 Pet. 1:17; Rev. 22:12). We should not feel that there is any contradiction between this teaching of reward and that of justification by faith alone. In the absolute sense those who have done all their duty can only describe themselves as 'unprofitable servants' (Lk. 17:10, AV) and whatever reward they receive as a gift of grace. Also it is

175

true that from the self-centred life, that is without repentance and faith and their fruits, there can come no service rendered as to the Lord from the heart, that he can reward.

Finally, as a link between verse 8 and verse 9 the words are added, *whether he is a slave or free.* This principle, like everything else that can be said of human duty before God and God's judgment of men and women applies to all alike, rich and poor, slave and free, servant and master. But it is to masters that the apostle must now speak.

9. *Do the same* to your servants, he says to the *masters,* thus making it clear that the same principles apply to them also. The outward actions required may be very different, but there is the same need to act towards servants 'as to the Lord' (v. 7), as doing 'the will of God' (v. 6), as showing 'good will' (v. 7), in fact, as servants have been called to act towards them. 'Consult their good as you expect them to consult yours' is the way that Moule (*ES*) paraphrases. Then a very practical point is touched on. *Threatening* came very easily to the lips of the master of slaves in the ancient world, and the slave could not answer back. It involved their 'trying to extort the last ounce of effort from their slaves by threat of punishment' (Mitton, *NCB*). The employer may still today speak and act as the one who has the 'whip-hand'. But Christian masters are reminded that all that they say or do to their servants must be said or done remembering that they have a Lord and *Master . . . in heaven.* To him they must give account, and not least of the way that they have treated those who have had to call them 'masters'. RSV accurately translates here, bringing out Paul's point that both servant and master stand ultimately on the same level, *he who is both their Master and yours is in heaven, and . . . there is no partiality with him.* To him both must give account. He watches over the relationship between them (*cf.* Jas. 5:1ff.). Servants have been told to render all their service as to a heavenly Lord. Masters are told to act towards their servants bearing in mind the fact that they are themselves servants, and the heavenly master is the one to whom they must give account. They have, moreover, the example that he himself set 'in the days of his flesh' (Heb. 5:7, AV) for all in positions of authority to follow (Jn. 13:13ff.). It is true that neither here nor in any other part of the New Testament is slavery denounced as a social system. In this section there is a greater concern for the quality of Christians' lives and service of others than of 'human rights'. Yet the Christian teaching of the equality of all men and women before an impartial God, and their relationships as brothers and sisters in Christ (Phm. 16), was the powerful force that was later to lead in one country after another to the abolition of slavery.[1]

VI. CONCLUSION (6:10–24)

A. THE CHRISTIAN CONFLICT (6:10–20)

10. *Finally* the apostle says, as he is about to bring his letter to a close. He has spoken of the greatness of the purpose of God in Christ, of the glory of his high calling, and the life that should follow from it. The standards have been set, the standards for personal life, for life in the fellowship of the Christian community, and in the more intimate circle of the home. Yet he wants still to remind his readers that such a life cannot be lived without a spiritual battle, of whose intensity he has become more and more conscious in his own experience. The one paramount necessity in this is the power of God. *Be strong*, or, more literally, 'be strengthened' (*cf.* Acts 9:22; Rom. 4:20; 2 Tim. 2:1). People cannot strengthen themselves; they must be empowered, and that not once for all but constantly, as the tense of the Greek indicates. Furthermore, he says, not 'by the Lord', though that would be true enough, but again *in the Lord*. When life is lived in union with him, within the orbit of his will and so of his grace, there need not be failure due to powerlessness (1 Jn. 2:14). Apart from him the Christian can do nothing (Jn. 15:1–5), but there is available all *the strength of his might*. This phrase brings us back to two of the words that have been used already in 1:19 (and a third, *dynamis*, is the verb that

---

[1] On the question of the attitude of the early church to slavery as an institution see J. B. Lightfoot, *St. Paul's Epistles to Colossians and to Philemon* (London, 1975). Swain, p. 99, makes the comment of the exhortation to masters, 'If Paul does not make a full frontal attack on slavery, he is certainly putting a time-bomb under it.'

he has employed), and the repetition gives the same emphasis on God's resources of prevailing, triumphant power as we noted in that passage.

11. Such strength is needed, for the conflict is fierce and long. But Paul now expresses in another way the equipping that the Christian needs – it is the *armour of God*, the *panoplia* (*cf.* 1 Thes. 5:8), the sum total of all the pieces of armour (*hopla*, Rom. 13:12) that he will describe in verses 14–17. The *armour of God* might mean that armour that God himself wears or that he supplies. Perhaps both were in mind. Day by day the apostle, at this time of his confinement (see on v. 20), was in all probability chained to a Roman soldier. His mind must often have turned from the thought of the soldier of Rome to the soldier of Jesus Christ, and from the soldier to whom he was bound to the heavenly warrior to whom his life was linked by more real, though invisible, bonds. As we shall see later in more detail, the description of the armour of the heavenly warrior, as given in Isaiah 59:17 (*cf.* Wisdom of Solomon 5:17–20), was in his mind; and Paul would have thought of the correspondence between the weapons of his armour and those given by him to the soldiers serving in the war under him. He would have thought too of the other details of the armour of the soldier at his side, and their counterparts in the provision for the Christian's spiritual conflict. These weapons that he is to describe are given that people *may be able to stand against the wiles of the devil. Stand* indeed is the keyword of the passage; for, as Moule puts it, 'the present picture is not of a march, or of an assault, but of the holding of the fortress of the soul and of the Church for the heavenly King' (*CB*). The same word is used for *the wiles of the devil* as has been used in 4:14 where he saw that it involved the idea of 'cunning devices'. This is the first indication of the difficulty of the fight. It is not just against the strength of man, but against the stratagems of a spiritual enemy, the subtle plans of the enemy of souls of which every experienced Christian warrior is well aware (*cf.* 2 Cor. 2:11).

12. The thought of a personal devil, though found in every part of the New Testament (*e.g.* Mt. 4:1–11; Jas. 4:7; 1 Pet. 5:8–9;

1 Jn. 5:18) does not commend itself in all quarters today. Still less does the idea of *the principalities* and *powers* of evil and spiritual *rulers of this present darkness*. But we should be slow to reject the biblical terms in which the spiritual life and its conflicts are spoken of, and realize rather that our vastly increased knowledge of the physical universe has not necessarily increased, and may in fact have dulled, our sense of the spiritual. We should be hesitant to regard ourselves as wiser than the apostles and our incarnate Lord concerning the unseen world. As Mitton (*NCB*) puts it, while many 'demythologise the word "devil" into a mere figure of speech for "evil",' others 'though acquainted with the theological difficulties in acknowledging a supreme evil being who is able to defy and thwart God, are also deeply aware of what appears to them as the skill and intelligence with which this mysterious force of evil campaigns to crush innocence and uprightness'. Men and women today feel themselves to be up against powers which, even if they describe them in material terms, are beyond their control, in spite of all their ability to penetrate the mysteries of the material universe and bring it into subjection. The interpretation of the *principalities* (Gk. *archai*) and *powers* (Gk. *exousiai*) by modern commentators to refer to 'socio-political structures of human society' as well as or instead of unseen spiritual forces must be considered here.[1] It is true that Paul uses the word *exousiai* for human powers (in Rom. 13:1–3), but here it seems that the stress is on the reality of a spiritual warfare. The enemies are not human (*flesh and blood*) although, of course, the spiritual powers of evil may use human instruments.

What is most important is that the apostle would not have his readers underestimate the power of the forces against them. We may bring out the emphasis of the original by translating, 'Not for us is the wrestling against flesh and blood'. Momentarily he would change from the figure of a soldier armed for battle to that of a wrestler; for the latter gives the stress he seeks to

[1] See E. Gordon Rupp, *Principalities and Powers: Studies in the Christian Conflict in History* (London, 1952), G. B. Caird, *Principalities and Powers* (Oxford, 1956), H. Berkhof, *Christ and the Powers* (Scottdale, 1962), J. H. Yoder, *The Politics of Jesus* (Grand Rapids, 1972), ch. 8; and for a critique, see P. T. O'Brien in *Biblical Interpretation and the Church*, ed. D. A. Carson (Exeter, 1984), ch. 5 and Stott, pp. 267ff.

convey on the personal nature of the conflict, and the reminder that guile as well as brute strength has to be faced. Then we have a list of synonyms similar to that of 1:21 for the spiritual forces that are the Christian's enemies, but the preposition is repeated with each as if to denote that 'each is to be dealt with severally' (Westcott). There is one word in the Greek (*kosmokratoras*) for *world rulers*. It can be used for one who is the ruler of the whole world, or for one whose authority is in the world, in the sense in which the devil is so described in John 12:31, 14:30 and 2 Corinthians 4:4. The world is frequently spoken of thus in the New Testament as in the power of the evil one (1 Jn. 5:19), and in consequence in *darkness* (*cf*. Lk. 22:53; Rom. 13:12; Col. 1:13). Those who, under the devil himself, hold such power in the world, and in consequence keep people in *darkness*, are those against whom Christians have to do battle. They are *the spiritual hosts of wickedness* and *against* them Christians are engaged in spiritual, not physical, conflict. Indeed as their own lives have been described as raised above this material world to 'the heavenly places' where they live 'in Christ' (2:6), so their spiritual conflict is there, and it is their spiritual possessions there (1:3) of which the powers of evil would try to rob them.

13. *Therefore*, Paul says, as you realize the grim power and resources of your spiritual foes, *take the whole armour of God*. Only at great peril can it be neglected. Three times he repeats now the word that has been used in verse 11, when he says that the great objective of the Christian warrior is to be able to *stand*. In fact the first use of the word in this verse is in the compound verb *withstand* (*antistēnai*; the simple verb is *stēnai*, 'stand') implying a stand against great opposition (*cf*. Jas. 4:7 and 1 Pet. 5:9, where the same word is applied to the same spiritual conflict). *The evil day*, to which particular reference is made, indicates a time when the conflict will be most severe, due both to persecution from without and trial from within the Christian fellowship. The apocalyptic passages of the Gospels (*e.g.* Mk. 13:4–23) and Paul in his letters (*e.g.* 2 Thes. 2:3) alike refer to the quickening of the conflict, the increase in intensity of the warfare, in a great crescendo, before the 'day of the Lord' comes (*cf*. 1 Jn. 2:18–19). For this in particular, as for every lesser 'evil day', the Christian must be prepared. There are many things to be done in the Christian's life, many opportunities of service, but Paul could see the possibility of a person doing great things, even the works of an apostle, and yet being a castaway in the end (1 Cor. 9:24–27). So he stresses here with all the emphasis he can, that *having done all*, having accomplished great things (as the verb implies), they must be sure *to stand* (*stēnai*).

14. *Stand therefore*, he says, in the armour provided, which alone will make you invincible. RSV *having girded your loins with truth* accurately translates the Greek participial phrase, showing the tense used, and conveying the sense of a deliberate personal action. The order in which the pieces of armour are described is the order in which the soldier would put them on. Strictly the girdle is not part of the armour, but before the armour can be put on the garments underneath must be bound together. The metaphor of girding is often used in the Bible because it describes a preparatory action necessary for a person with the flowing garments of those days before work could be done, a race run, or a battle fought (*e.g.* see Lk. 12:35; 1 Pet. 1:13). Isaiah 59:17 and the description of the Christian's armour in 1 Thessalonians 5:8 do not mention the girdle, but Isaiah 11:5 says of the 'shoot from the stump of Jesse' (Is. 11:1) that 'Righteousness shall be the girdle of his waist, and faithfulness the girdle of his loins'. We may conclude that it is not the truth of the gospel that is alluded to, but the undergirding of *truth* in the sense of 'integrity', 'truth in the inward being' of which Psalm 51:6 speaks. As 'the girdle . . . gives ease and freedom of movement', so 'it is the truth which gives this freedom with ourselves, with our neighbours and with God. Lack of perfect sincerity hampers us at every turn'.[1]

Secondly, there is *the breastplate of righteousness* which must be *put on*. This description comes from that of the heavenly warrior in Isaiah 59:17, and this fact, as well as the reference of 2 Corinthians 6:7 to 'the weapons of righteousness for the right hand and for the left', seems to indicate that what was in the

[1]H. L. Goudge, *Three Lectures on the Epistle to the Ephesians* (1920), p. 76.

apostle's mind at this point was not the righteousness of God which is imputed to us (Rom. 3:21–22), that means our justification and the forgiveness of our sins; but, as Calvin, Westcott, Moule and many others take it, uprightness of character, 'loyalty in principle and action to the holy law of God' (Moule, *CB*). To neglect what we know to be righteous action is to leave a gaping hole in our armour. We may compare this use of the word *righteousness* with that in 5:9 and in Romans 6:13 and 14:17.

15. Thirdly, Paul says *having shod your feet with the equipment of the gospel of peace*. The word translated *equipment* can have two quite different meanings. It may be 'preparedness', and some, taking this as the right meaning here, assume that although defence is primarily in the apostle's mind in his description of the Christian conflict in this passage, he cannot just think of Christians defending themselves. They must go forward with *the gospel*. Part of their necessary *equipment*, therefore, is the readiness at any moment to take out the good news *of peace* to others. It has been argued that the apostle's thought has moved from Isaiah 59 to Isaiah 52:7, which was in his mind in 2:17. Another meaning of the Greek noun *hetoimasia*, however, is 'preparation' in the sense of a 'prepared foundation', and thus it appears to be used in the Greek of Psalm 89:14 (88:15 in LXX). This would give the meaning here that the knowledge of the dependence on *the gospel* that gives a person *peace* in heart and life is a necessary *equipment* (like the hobnailed sandals of the Roman soldier) if he is to have a firm foothold in the conflict. So NEB: 'let the shoes on your feet be the gospel of peace, to give you firm footing'. This second meaning fits the context better, with its dominant thought of being able to stand unmoved against the foe. Even so the words used carry the hint that warfare is not the complete description of Christians' occupation – they are also messengers with good news. There is also what Harnack called a 'lofty paradox',[1] that *the gospel of peace* can be spoken of in a context which emphasizes the grim reality of the Christian's warfare.

---

[1] A. von Harnack, *Militia Christi* (Tübingen, 1905), p. 13.

16. Next, 'to cover all the rest' (Scott), comes *the shield*, the large oblong *scutum* shaped like a door (and the Gk. word *thyreos* used for *shield* comes from the word for 'door') which in effect did cover much of the body. *The shield* is *faith*, by which – as in 1 Thessalonians 5:8 when Paul speaks of 'faith and love' as the breastplate – he means reliance on God. 'The true safeguard in the evil day', Moule says, 'lies ever, not in introspection, but in that look wholly outward, Godward, which is the essence of faith (see Ps. xxv:15)' (*CB*). A glimpse of the enemy is again thought necessary. In New Testament times darts were often made with tow dipped in pitch and then set on fire, and the wooden shield needed to be covered with leather so as to quench them quickly. The 'wiles of the devil' (v. 11) Paul knew to include such *flaming darts*, people's arrow tongues, the shafts of impurity, selfishness, doubt, fear, disappointment, that are planned by the enemy to burn and destroy. The apostle knew that only faith's reliance on God could *quench* and deflect such weapons whenever they were hurled at the Christian. It is of interest also to recall that the Romans had a system of locking these large shields together for their corporate defence against their enemies and for attack.

17. *Take the helmet of salvation*, Paul says next, and the verb used is especially appropriate to salvation as a gift of God. It implies also that *salvation* is a provision for men and women that can as definitely be received as any other part of the Christian armour. The soul's deliverance is not a matter of uncertainty to the end. In Isaiah 59:17 the divine warrior wears 'the helmet of salvation' as the worker and bringer of salvation. For Christians, *salvation* is part of the defensive armour that is essential for their safety in the fray. It may be taken as God's gift of salvation from the penalty of sin, but even more as his saving help to protect from the power of sin, and the parallel in 1 Thessalonians 5:8 suggests that here also we may take it to include 'the hope' of final deliverance from the very presence of sin. Without that hope to fortify, without the present deliverance, and the confidence of rescue from the bondage of the past, the Christian may easily be mortally wounded in the conflict. Psalm 140:7 is a significant parallel to the thought of this verse: 'O Lord, my

Lord, my strong deliverer, thou hast covered my head in the day of battle'.

Finally there is *the sword of the Spirit*. The Old Testament often refers to speech as a sword. The words of the wicked are said to wound as a sword (*e.g.* Pss. 57:4; 64:3). But in the Bible God's own *word*[1] is also as a *sword* in his hand, a sword that lays bare, separating the false from the true (Heb. 4:12), bringing judgment (Is. 11:4; Ho. 6:5) but also bringing salvation. His word can thus be wielded by his messengers in the lives of others (*e.g.* Is. 49:2), but here the thought is of *the word of God* as a defensive weapon for the person who holds it. The genitives in the preceding verses have been genitives of apposition, and some have taken this here to mean that *the Spirit* himself is *the sword*. Clearly, however, what the sword stands for is explained, not by the genitive, but by the following clause. The word is the Spirit's sword,[2] because given by the Spirit (*cf.* 3:5; 2 Tim. 3:16; Heb. 3:7; 9:8; 10:15; 1 Pet. 1:11; 2 Pet. 1:21) and it is 'as He works in the believer as the Spirit of truth (Joh. xiv:17) and faith (2 Cor. iv:13). He puts the sword into his grasp and enables him to use it' (Moule, *CB*). The Lord's use of the word of Scripture in his temptations (Mt. 4:1–10) is sufficient illustration and incentive for Christians to fortify themselves with the knowledge and understanding of *the word* that they may with similar conviction and power defend themselves by it in the onslaughts of the enemy.

18. Prayer cannot quite be described as a part of the armour, but the description of the Christian's equipment for the conflict cannot but include reference to prayer. RSV begins a new sentence with this verse, but the Greek has a participle, 'praying', which may in fact be taken with all the foregoing commands. The different parts of the armour have been described, and in effect the apostle would say 'Each piece put on with prayer',[3]

---

[1]The Greek *rhema* is used in this verse, but reference to a concordance shows that both this word and the Greek word *logos* are often used in this same sense in the New Testament.

[2]The reference is not only to Scripture, but to all 'words that come from God' (NEB) by his Spirit; we, however, naturally think of the application to God's word in the Bible as *the sword of the Spirit*.

[3]From *Stand up, stand up for Jesus* by George Duffield.

and then continue still in *all prayer and supplication*. The word *all* or its equivalent is used four times in this one verse in the original. As Barth (*AB*) puts it, 'Nothing less is suggested than that the life and strife of the saints be one great prayer to God, that this prayer be offered in ever new forms however good or bad the circumstances, and that this prayer not be self-centred but express the need and hope of all the saints.' The New Testament frequently exhorts Christians not to cease from prayer (*e.g.* Lk. 18:1; Rom. 12:12; Phil. 4:6; Col. 4:2; 1 Thes. 5:17), and here the particular point is that every incident of life (*kairos* is the word used – see on 1:10 and 5:16) is to be dealt with in prayer. The apostle is aware that this is no light demand to be made. People very easily take their difficulties to their fellows instead of to God. 'The power of prayer is gained by systematic discipline' Westcott wisely says. Constancy in prayer and the natural recourse of the Christian to prayer come only as prayer has become a habit of life, and as a person has learnt to *keep alert with all perseverance*. *Keep alert* or 'watch' was frequently the exhortation of Jesus himself to his disciples, and most significantly at the time when they needed to find strength by prayer for their hour of trial in Gethsemane.

But again there is a wonderful balance in Paul's presentation. Even this watchfulness and discipline is not just a matter of human striving; for true Christian prayer is prayer *in the Spirit*. The Spirit is given as helper, and not least for the task of prayer (Rom. 8:26–27); but as in the case of the other uses of this phrase in the Greek in this letter (2:18, 22; 3:5; 5:18) *in the Spirit* means more than by the Spirit's help. The Spirit is the atmosphere of Christians' lives, and as they live *in the Spirit* grace will be given to watch and power to continue in prayer.

Such prayer, Paul says finally, unlimited in the times and the ways in which it may be offered, is to be unlimited in outreach to those for whom it is offered. Christians are not to think only of their own spiritual conflict, but to be concerned for the whole church of Christ, and for the victory of all their fellows in the fight (*cf.* 1 Tim. 2:1). There is a similar thought in 1 Peter 5:9, where those who are called to resist the devil are reminded that their 'brother Christians are going through the same kinds of suffering' (NEB) 'throughout the world' (RSV).

19. At this point, as Paul has asked prayer for others, he cannot forbear to ask his readers' earnest supplication for him. As he prayed for the churches, he constantly asked their prayers for him (*e.g.* Col. 4:3; 1 Thes. 5:25; 2 Thes. 3:1). He was aware of his position in the forefront of the battle, even though he was in prison, and of his vulnerability. His great desire was not that they should pray for his liberation, but rather that they should intercede for the great ministry of the word that was his still. Two things he craved for the task: wisdom and boldness, clarity and courage in proclaiming the message. He asks them to pray *that utterance may be given me in opening my mouth.* '"Opening the mouth" is an expression used only where some grave utterance is in question,' says Abbott. Paul is always conscious of his great responsibility in being entrusted with the gospel of eternal salvation, and so he desires above all that whenever he has opportunity to speak that gospel God will give him the words (*cf.* Ps. 51:15). Furthermore, as he is aware that by God's grace he has been given understanding in *the mystery of the gospel* (see on 3:3–4 and 9), so he needs constantly to be given power *to proclaim* it *boldly,* without in any way departing from or diminishing 'the whole counsel of God' (Acts 20:27), whether for the sake of the praise of others, or to avoid their scorn or opposition. Like the early apostles (Acts 4:29) his prayer was not for success, nor for deliverance from danger or suffering, but for boldness in proclaiming the gospel of God that was entrusted to him.

20. Up to this point the apostle has said little about himself, except to remind his readers twice that it is from his prison confinement he is exhorting, pleading, praying (3:1; 4:1). Now, in order to give point to their prayers, he reminds them more specifically of his condition. He is *an ambassador in chains.* He was aware of the many ambassadors who came to Rome from far and near; he, though in prison at the will of the powerful Roman emperor, felt the dignity and tremendous importance of his position as representative of the King of kings. He was the bearer of the word of his royal master, the word that entreated people who were at enmity against him to be reconciled to him (2 Cor. 5:20). Because of the way that he has thus represented his Lord, he was *in chains*. This expression *en halusei* probably, though not quite certainly, indicates the manner of his imprisonment. In Acts 28:16 it is said that when Paul first came to Rome he 'was allowed to stay by himself, with the soldier that guarded him', and then in verse 20 of that same chapter he tells the Jews that 'because of the hope of Israel' he is 'bound with this chain' (*tēn halysin tautēn perikeimai*). He speaks as he does of his imprisonment not to excite feelings of sympathy in his readers. 'What concerns Paul most . . . is not that his wrist may be unchained, but that his mouth may be opened in testimony; not that he may be set free, but that the gospel may spread freely and without hindrance' (Stott). Imprisonment brings its own special temptation to bow to the fear of what those with political power may do. Paul knows that he has a responsibility (and a privilege), which remains his to the end of his life. He knows how he *ought to speak* in bearing witness to the gospel. Therefore he repeats the request that they pray that he *may declare* that gospel *boldly*.

B. FINAL MESSAGE AND GREETING (6:21-24)

21-22. The apostle has some final personal words, and these are very closely similar to Colossians 4:7-9, and in the Introduction[1] we have considered the significance of this fact. If we have rightly judged the whole setting and purpose of this letter, the apostle has refrained from personal allusions, either to himself or to his readers, in order to give it a wider usefulness among the churches of Asia. But there are strong personal links that bind him to most of these churches. As by different means he has heard news of them, he would now convey news of his own affairs and circumstances. There may have been special need for this because of their anxiety for him (*cf.* Phil. 1:12), and on account of their temptation to be discouraged by his imprisonment (see on 3:13). The force of the *you* could be that he, having heard of their affairs, was giving them opportunity for their part of knowing his. If, however, he had just written the conclusion

[1]See pp. 26-27.

to Colossians, he might naturally write in this way, without a moment's thought whether or not the readers of this letter would be aware of the other that he had written for Colossae.

Tychicus was Paul's messenger, whom he could call a *beloved brother and faithful minister* (see on 3:7), and he adds now, for the last time in the letter, the phrase that conditions all true Christian living and service and relationships, *in the Lord*. *Tychicus* is the bearer of Colossians and, inevitably, of Philemon too. We first hear of him as one of the representatives of the Asian church who went with Trophimus from Greece and presumably on to Jerusalem at the end of Paul's third missionary journey (Acts 20:4; and see also 21:29). In Titus 3:12 Paul speaks of sending him or Artemas to Titus, while 2 Timothy 4:12 refers to him as actually sent to Ephesus from Rome, by which it is implied that he was one of those who served faithfully with Paul in his last trying days. There are traditions, but by no means an agreed tradition, concerning his work as a bishop in later days. The *purpose* at this time of sending one so close to him as Tychicus was that he might give accurate news, and by that news, and no doubt by other spiritual exhortation, he might *encourage* their *hearts*.

23. There follows a greeting, which like that of the very beginning (see on 1:2) is a true prayer. Paul picks up the three great qualities of the Christian life, the three blessings, of which he has said so much in this letter, and prays that his readers may possess them. *Peace* – peace with God, peace in the heart, peace with one another – *be to the brethren*. Then *love with faith*. In one sense love springs from faith, and without faith's union with Christ love cannot begin to grow. Faith in the sense of faithfulness (see on 1:1), however, is a fruit of love. All come *from God the Father*, the source of all, *and the Lord Jesus Christ*, who is mediator to us of every spiritual blessing that we can have (1:3).

24. Now the final prayer is for *Grace*, the grace with which the letter began, and which has been the theme of the whole. It is noteworthy that when the word is used in the opening greeting of the letters it is regularly without the article in the Greek, but when it stands in a closing prayer the article is used (*cf.* 2 Cor.

13:14; Col. 4:18; 1 Tim. 6:21; 2 Tim. 4:22; Tit. 3:15; Heb. 13:25). Perhaps we should see the influence of the liturgical form of a closing prayer being used even at this time in Christian worship. Perhaps the implication is just that it is 'the grace about which I have said so much'. When he qualifies the *all* who are recipients of grace by the words *who love our Lord Jesus Christ* it is not with a desire to suggest an exclusiveness of divine grace, but with the reminder that only where there is answering love can the love and grace of God continue to be received in their full and wonderful measure.

The variety of the translations of the final phrase of the letter, *en aphtharasia*, reveals the difficulty of being sure of its meaning. *Aphtharsia* is used for 'incorruptibility' in the sense of immortality in Romans 2:7, 2 Timothy 1:10 and elsewhere. Thus RSV translates, *love undying*. The word, however, can suggest a moral incorruptibility; hence the AV rendering 'in sincerity'. The phrase, however, may be taken in quite a different way, as belonging with God's grace ('grace with immortality') rather than to speak of the quality of human love that responds to divine grace. Thus NEB, 'God's grace be with all who love our Lord Jesus Christ, grace and immortality.' Mitton (*NCB*) comments on its being an appropriate ending to a letter which has said so much of God's grace; 'this grace will never fail them . . . It is not subject to change and decay'. On the other hand, as the love of God is an eternal love, it is understandable that the love that answers it should be kept up unfailingly (1 Cor. 13:8) and shine more and more brightly to the perfect day of God.